THE PRAYER OF THE OPPRESSED

الدُّعَاءُ النَّاصِرِيُّ

Imam Muḥammad b. Nāṣir al-Darʿī's

THE PRAYER of THE OPPRESSED

THE SWORD OF VICTORY'S LOT
OVER EVERY TYRANNY AND PLOT

Translated and Introduced by

Hamza Yusuf

SANDALA

Published by Sandala Productions Inc., 2010.

First edition 2010.
Printed in the United States of America.

ISBN - 978-1-4507-0608-7

Cover Photograph: Mikhail Evstafiev
This photograph, taken in 1995, shows a Chechen man praying during the battle of Grozny.

Cover Design and Layout: Abdallateef Whiteman
Calligraphy: Elinor Aishah Holland

Editor: Safir Ahmed
Arabic Editors: Shaykh Jamal Zahabi and Hisham Mahmoud
Managing Editor: Uzma Fatima Husaini
Copy Editor: Tom Devine
Poetry Editors: Daniel Abdal-Hayy Moore and Tom Devine
CD Production: Abdallateef Whiteman

بسم الله الرحمن الرحيم

IN THE NAME OF GOD,
THE BENEFICENT, THE MERCIFUL

قَالَ رَسُولُ اللهِ صَلَّى اللهُ عَلَيْهِ وَسَلَّمَ نَاقِلاً عَنْ رَبِّهِ عَزَّ وَجَلَّ
اِشْتَدَّ غَضَبِي عَلَى مَنْ ظَلَمَ مَنْ لَمْ يَجِدْ نَاصِراً غَيْرِي

Fierce is My wrath upon the one who oppresses anyone
who can find no ally other than Me.

— GOD

The Prophet Muḥammad ﷺ once said to us,
"Help your brother, the oppressor and the oppressed."
We asked, "O Messenger of God, we understand how we can help one oppressed, but how should we help one who is oppressing?"
"By stopping him from oppressing others," he replied.

– IMAM AL-BUKHĀRĪ'S HADITH COLLECTION, 9TH CENTURY

It is not that you should invoke the wrath of God upon an oppressor, but rather the essence of this affair is that you should implore God to guide the oppressor that he might leave his tyranny and redress the wrongs he has committed or beg the forgiveness of those whom he has wronged. Surely, that God should guide one lost soul due to your prayers should be worth more to you than all that the sun rises upon.

– SĪDĪ AḤMAD ZARRŪQ'S COMMENTARY ON *AL-WAGHLISIYYAH*, 15TH CENTURY

Foolish men imagine that because judgment for an evil thing is delayed, there is no justice, but an accidental one, here below. Judgment for an evil thing is many times delayed some day or two, some century or two; but it is sure as life, it is sure as death!

– THOMAS CARLYLE, *PAST AND PRESENT*, 1843

Dedication

To Rachel Corrie, a gentle lamb who resisted the oppressor without hatred or rancor in her heart and paid the ultimate price; to Chris Hedges and all those who have, despite its political incorrectness, stood by the Palestinian people in their just cause; to the people of Darfur; to the six million victims of the 21st century holocaust of the Congo; to the Kashmiris, Iraqis, Afghans, Chechnyans, and every other victim of the many tragic oppressions I have witnessed in my lifetime; to victims of oppression everywhere whose only weapon is the power of prayer, this work is humbly dedicated.

Table of Contents

Introduction
1

A Reflection on Divine Love
33

About the Author
39

About This Translation and Recording
47

License to Transmit
50

The Prayer of the Oppressed
53

Transliterated Text
77

Appendix on Intercession
97

Transliteration Key
102

Acknowledgments
104

Introduction

If a man is slain unjustly, his heir shall be entitled to satisfaction. But let him not carry his vengeance to excess, for his victim is sure to be assisted and avenged. – QUR'AN, 17:33

Limit your hostility toward your enemy, for one day he may become your beloved. – PROPHET MUḤAMMAD ﷺ

It is strange that we should not realize that no enemy could be more dangerous to us than the hatred with which we hate him, and that by our efforts against him we do less damage to our enemy than is wrought in our own heart. – ST. AUGUSTINE

The last sphere to be conquered by the spirit of justice is the sphere of reactive feelings. – FRIEDRICH NIETZSCHE

THE WORLD IS FILLED with wonders, and nature exhibits order and perfection. Stars follow a calculable course, seasons come with the exactitude of clockwork, and all life on earth reveals undeniable design and divine generosity. Each creature knows its place in the natural order and follows similar patterns of embryonic development, birth, growth, decay, and finally death. Beasts of prey take only what they need to survive from weaker ones, none oppressing the other, never guilty of massacres or capricious killings, all living together, from our perspective, in a world of harmony and mutual understanding. The Qur'an says, "There is not an animal on the earth nor a bird that flies upon two wings except they form communities like you. We have omitted nothing from the Book, and then all shall be gathered to their Lord" (6:38).

Human beings, too, live largely in structured societies of immense complexity that fulfill the many needs and aspirations of men and women in their daily lives and provide avenues for both their individual and collective pursuits. Each person, in seeking a livelihood, helps others to fulfill their needs. Commenting on this veiled but vital aspect of humanity, the 10th century Arab poet, al-Mutanabbī (d. 354/965), said:

Men, though separate, need one another;
Without knowing, each serves the other.

While our collective social organization is premised on order, balance, and mutual respect, we are also imbued with the capacity to violate that very order and balance. Men, like animals, are part of the natural world, but, unlike animals, betray in their actions a nature wholly incongruous with Nature. We breach natural laws in our thoughts, emotions, desires, and diets. Instead of loving people and using objects, we love objects and use people. We strive for our own success through aggression, by enviously and consciously undermining the success of others. We feel slighted easily and forgive with great difficulty; we desire far more than we use, eat much more than we need, lust too often, and love too seldom; we pursue luxury for ourselves and neglect those in need. Indeed, pride, envy, wrath, greed, sloth, gluttony, and lust sometimes seem to be the defining traits of our species. These "deadly sins" were once despised, denounced, and disciplined. Yet, unlike our ancestors, our advertisers pander with pride to these human weaknesses; they are now packaged for display to please our eyes, tease our tongues, and seduce our hearts and minds.

Men and women have always struggled with temptation. But what is different today is how acceptable it has become, in the name of commerce, to publicly prey on the human weaknesses of others and to entice them to indulge in their whims and cave in to their cravings. But where have all these efforts brought us? What exactly have they wrought? Individually, our hunger increases as our happiness diminishes, and collectively, conflict and war plague our world, making the panacea of peace seem more distant than ever.

This predicament is largely a result of our ignorance of the nature of good and evil—because we often cannot distinguish between the two, we are unable to use our intellect to see clearly and make choices (*intelligere* literally means "to choose among"). Thus, we grope in the dark in pursuit of false desires. And these insatiable appetites, crass cravings, and pitiful pursuits, in turn, often lead us to oppress others.

THE CYCLE OF OPPRESSION

Oppression is almost universally understood to be a crime that involves an "action on another's person or property without authority or permission." Some simply define it as "putting something where it does not belong," whether it is one's hands, genitals, army, wealth, or anything else. It arises when a moral agent violates either societal standards of justice as in customary law, secular standards as in positive law and natural law, or revealed standards as in religious law. Interestingly, all legal and ethical perspectives agree on this point much more than they disagree.

But where does the desire to oppress come from? What is its genesis? What feeds or incites oppressive acts? The Qur'an states the following: "If God expanded provisions for mortals, they would surely act unjustly on earth; but God sends down what God wills in a measured way. For God is aware, watchful of all humanity" (42:27). A profound truth about the psychological nature of those who oppress is discernable in this verse: oppression is largely driven by power and wealth. An Arab proverb states, "Those who possess, oppress." In another verse, the Qur'an states, "Surely man transgresses when he deems himself independent" (96:6-7). The insightful dictum of the English historian, Lord Acton (d. 1902), still rings true: "Power tends to corrupt, but absolute power corrupts absolutely." Conversely, however, absolute powerlessness appears to have the same corrosive effect. Between these two extremes swirls a seemingly unbreakable cycle of oppression.

Far more potent than power and wealth in this vicious cycle are hate and resentment, which exacerbate the insidious effects of oppression on the souls of both the oppressor and the oppressed. The oppressor must hate his victims in order to rationalize his behavior, and so free himself from cognitive dissonance. In having the innate knowledge that what he is doing is wrong, he is confronted with two options: use the defense mechanism of denial, or stop doing what is wrong. A third option is rarely afforded the tyrant: that of another restraining him from his tyranny and liberating him with compassion. What occurs, more often than not, however, is that the oppressor degrades and vilifies his victims, thereby licensing his wrongful acts in his own mind.

Unfortunately, the oppressed also do their part in perpetuating the cycle of oppression. Often, due to the oppressed people's helplessness and frustration in defending themselves against their aggressor, a deep resentment begins to take root in their hearts. This resentment either poisons them entirely or bursts forth in an aggressive attempt to purge the body politic through the redressing of wrongs. Too often, the purging spirals into a bloodletting, and the bitter cycle continues. Hate, aggression, and violence beget more of the same.

THE NATURE OF THE TYRANT

The Qur'an describes the oppressor or tyrant as one who is "deaf, dumb, and blind," which is, in essence, the spiritual reality of the tyrant. He cannot hear the cries of his victims; he cannot commune with those he is oppressing, for he views them imperiously as belonging to a lesser order of being than himself, and thus simply as exploitable commodities or, worse, a pestilence to be purged; and he cannot see the harm he inflicts. Aristotle (d. 322 BCE) reminds us that all tyrants invariably surround themselves with sycophants because they cannot bear to hear the truth. But the tyrant also needs these yes-men because he demands tacit approval of his beliefs and actions, and what he fears most is an honest and critical look at himself. The more a tyrant's power increases, the less he tolerates dissent. And what is true for a tyrant is also true for a tyrannical nation.

He demands that all agree with him and confirm his position because he can see, hear, or speak to no other but himself. He believes that his sight is clear, his understanding is unsurpassed, and his words, and only his words, are worthy of utterance or consideration. As human beings, it is only through others that we can truly see ourselves, hear ourselves, and speak to ourselves; but in his self-obsession, a tyrant is utterly incapable of such reflection. The example of Pharaoh, the archetypal tyrant in both the Bible and the Qur'an, best illustrates this point, with the Qur'an's reference to his statement, "I am your lord, most high" (79:24). This statement captures a certain truth about the nature of the oppressor: he is an idolater, one who has chosen to worship his self rather than his Creator. His actions evince this, should his tongue fail to express it; and because he sees himself as a god in place of God, he is not to be crossed or confronted without the exacting of a terrible price.

This lack of vision, however, afflicts not only the oppressor's eye, but his heart as well, because at its core, it is an introspective myopia. In another verse, the Qur'an explains, "It is not the eyes that go blind, but the hearts within the breasts that go blind" (22:46). And this reveals another important facet of the nature of the oppressor: Deep down, he is an infantile self, a pathetic child trapped in an egocentric world. When he inflicts pain and suffering on others, he feels no remorse because he has no sense of the other. The entire world, from his mother's breast to the far horizon, is but an extension of his self, an amplification of his own image. He is essentially undifferentiated and thus unable to see any suffering except his own. He has not entered into a spiritual version of what the 20th century French psychoanalyst Jacques Lacan (d.1981) termed the "mirror stage," during which an infant learns to differentiate itself from the world and begins to recognize there are discernable others who exist "out there." Through the mirror of the other, we see our selves. In failing to do so, we fail to develop our individuality.

The Prophet Muḥammad ﷺ said, "The believer is a mirror for another believer." In other words, the believer sees himself in others. The tyrant, however, is not individuated from others in the spiritual sense; he is unable to see all as himself, and thus to love all and wish good for all, as the Qur'anic verse explains: "Your creation and your resurrection are as one soul" (31:28). Rather, the tyrant exists as a sentient—and central—being; all others are merely a supporting cast, and everything exists simply to serve as a prop in the epic drama that is his life.

In modern parlance, the tyrant is a sociopath, an individual who functions in society with a surface rationality that masks an utter lack of social and personal responsibility. He is concerned only with his own gratification, even if it is gained through the pain of others. Indeed, he does not feel their pain, because, in his mind, they do not really exist as conscious creatures. Only by allowing meaning to penetrate our souls do we acquire the capacity for remorse. To understand is to realize our responsibility—literally, our "ability to respond." This is what the "deaf, dumb, and blind" tyrant is incapable of doing, and why calamity is the greatest gift God can bestow upon him.

Calamity brings the tyrant to his knees, lays him low, and humbles him, causing him to engage in introspection and to see the reality of his inner self. In gaining self-knowledge, we are able to feel remorse, and through remorse, we are granted entry into the kingdom of heaven. Through the gift of discerning sight, we can see that God exists and realize that our existence is wholly dependent upon His will; through the gift of attentive listening, we can hear God's call, which can help us mute the cacophonic noise of our obsessions and preoccupations; and with the gift of mindful speech, we can respond to God's call with contrition in our own voice, offering the Divine that which only we possess—our nothingness and our need.

THE TYRANT WITHIN US

One aspect too often overlooked in attempts to understand oppressors is the common, everyday manifestation of the tyrant. We look at the larger-than-life tyrants of history, the ancient despots, or the moderns like Hitler, Stalin, Tito, and Saddam, and in our preoccupation with them, we fail to acknowledge that a little bit of the tyrant exists in all of us, albeit a subtle one. Subtle tyrants often mask themselves under a veneer of decency. Thus, our tyrannical nature is generally hidden, but it reveals itself in small ways in our daily existence: our attitudes toward others; the way we treat our children or our spouse, dominating them in quiet but cruel ways; the obsequiousness we display toward our superiors and the contempt in which we hold our subordinates. And it reigns, also, in our inner world of perceptions, opinions, ideas, and prejudices.

Human beings have been honored in being invited into a divine covenant to act as caretakers of God's dominion, not rule as tyrants over it. Indeed, this responsibility of stewardship is so grave that the Qur'an states that the heavens, the earth, and the mountains all refused it, fearful of failing at the task: "We presented the trust to the heavens and the earth and the mountains, but they declined to bear it out of grief for its consequences; but man took it upon himself, for he is unjust and ignorant..." (33:72).

And when we betray this trust, we are indeed both unjust and ignorant. Earthly power is contingent, not absolute; it is a sacred trust from God for the purpose of serving humanity. The one entrusted with such power must fulfill that trust with equity and fairness, or else it leads to oppression.

An oppressor burdens others, smothering them under the weight of tyranny. The oppressed could be one's children, spouse, employees, subjects, neighbors, or community. Oppression takes many forms. The thief oppresses by taking advantage of his victims' inability to constantly police their property. The rapist oppresses by taking advantage of the physical weakness of his victim.

Oppression is a form of injustice, and injustice always occurs from an abuse of power, hidden or manifest. Power is God's alone, and thus any power entrusted to us is only to be used with servitude. Yet the tyrant usurps this power, deeming it his own, and behaves arbitrarily and capriciously.

CALAMITIES AND THE VIRTUE OF PATIENCE

The Qur'an demands that we see calamities as the fruit of our own tyranny, and recognize that our suffering is rooted in our attachment to all that is other than God. For calamities compel us to acknowledge our dependence upon our Creator; they force us to see that we need to offer our servitude to none other than God alone. When we recognize this, we are liberated from the oppression of both the self and others, and whatever befalls us reveals itself as a tribulation from the sole source of all that was, is, and ever will be. The Qur'an states: "Those who when calamities befall them say, 'We belong to God alone, and to God we return'—these are the ones who have grace from their Lord and mercy" (2:156-157).

"We belong to God," indeed, and anything God wants to do with us should be acceptable to us as servants in a state of submission. In Arabic, the first part of the phrase "*innā li l-lāhi wa innā ilayhi rājiʿūn*" uses *lām* (*li*), the particle of possession, thus indicating that we are possessions of God, and one does not question the actions of any owner regarding his possessions. It is for us to simply accept what God does with His property. This is not to imply that there is no room for questioning or reflection—rather, the distinction is that, if we question, as the angels did concerning the placing of Adam ﷷ as vicegerent in the earth, it must only be to *understand*, not to object, for we have no standing to do so. While this is difficult for the modern mind to fathom, it is the essence of Abrahamic submission, profoundly illustrated in the Akedah of his first born, which the Qur'an describes as a great tribulation for Abraham ﷺ.

God promises a reward without measure in the next world to those who are patient with tribulations in this one. This does not mean that we should adhere to a passive quietism, refraining from attempts to redress wrongs or oppose injustice; rather, it means we must strive for an inner world of submission and resignation even as we struggle to restore balance and restitution to the outer world. In this lies a subtle distinction lost on too many.

Another subtle distinction, also ignored or forgotten, is the intended goal: While the Qur'an commands us to work toward social justice, we are not responsible for the *outcome* of our efforts; in opposing injustice, we are accountable *only* for the struggle itself. For it is this struggle, and the knowledge that it is a trial from God, that allows our soul to be protected from dissolution, and from the spiritual entropy that reduces men to cynics who resent the world, surrender to its wrongs, or, worse, become participants in them. This knowledge also prevents those engaged in a genuine struggle from using means that betray the ends, however tempting or efficacious those means may be. Too many activists or victims of oppression succumb to bitter resentment when this truth is not rooted in their hearts.

Resentment ultimately stems from a complete dissatisfaction with the world or aspects of it, and is, therefore, dissatisfaction with God. This diabolic blame-game can only result in one's blaspheming, like the devil himself, against God. In the Qur'anic narrative, Satan says to God, "For leading me astray, I will misguide all of Your servants, save the sincere among them [over whom I have no control]" (15:39-40). He then tempts both Adam and Eve ﷺ into partaking of the forbidden fruit, resulting in what is commonly referred to as their "Fall." However, according to the Qur'an, God's vicegerents, Adam and Eve ﷺ, unlike Satan, take full responsibility for their actions and blame neither each other nor the devil for their wrongdoing, even though it was the devil who beguiled them into eating of the tree. According to the Islamic tradition, in resisting the temptation to place blame elsewhere, they restored their state of sanctity with their Lord (7:20-23). In order for an individual to hold the lofty position of God's vicegerent, he or she must learn to take responsibility. This is a leader's fate. If, as human beings, we are to rule the earth in the shadow of divine authority, then we must be willing to accept full responsibility, even for that for which we are not wholly liable. Both Adam and Eve ﷺ were worthy of being God's representatives on earth because they accepted culpability and contritely asked God's forgiveness. And in God's unhesitating response, and, thus, in their "Fall," lay the elevation of humanity.

The Prophet Muḥammad ﷺ said, "Whoever finds good, let him praise God, and whoever finds other than that, let him only blame himself." The essence of this statement is not a negation of oppression or a declaration that there is no absolute and objective right and wrong in the world. On the contrary, Islam affirms justice and establishes lucid criteria for right and wrong. In his statement, what the Prophet ﷺ is sharing with us is the profound secret that the world and our experience of it is, in reality, contained in our own *perception*. That is, if we are connected with God, then even in calamities, we find good. In other words, if we find "other than" good in the world, we are missing something fundamental to our faith. Those who are consciously aware, at all times, of God's sovereignty in all matters cannot be manipulated, for they know, in truth, that *all* is from God—not just the sweetness of blessings, but also the bitter cup of tribulation. Ultimately, it is our response to the world that determines our state with our Creator. As John Milton (d. 1674) put it:

> The mind is its own place, and in itself,
> Can make a Heaven of Hell, a Hell of Heaven.

Once we know this, like all of the prophets before us, we can take on the sins of the world and forgive others, and thus guide others. Their sins are a tribulation for us, just as ours are a tribulation for them. In this, we are all responsible for our collective sins. We will be asked how we "responded" to them: with patience, resignation, repentance, and restitution? Or with disquietude, anger, resentment, and further injustice?

The cycles of violence that now hold much of humanity in a death-grip can only be abated if each of us is willing to acknowledge that the oppressor and the oppressed are both dimensions of our own selves. We are actually reflections of each other.

The Qur'an reminds us: "We have made each of you a trial for the other; will you show patience?" (25:20). In today's vernacular, the first part translates to "hell is other people." Ironically, the one who deems other people his hell is very often *theirs*. Only the saint is freed from this, and is content, for the sake of God, to bear the hell presented by people in this world, in order to free himself from Hell in the next one. In fact, he ascends to higher ground and provides others, through the vehicle of his own sanctified character, a glimpse of Heaven on earth. God's simple question—"Will you show patience?"—is not rhetorical. It speaks to this truth, underscoring the fact that showing patience in the face of other people's hell, and not only bearing it, but also recompensing its evil with our own good character, is our challenge and what we are called upon to do.

Patience is neither resignation nor fatalism. It is the quality that prevents outer circumstances from dictating our inner states. It is freeing ourselves of the reactionary mind and the Pavlovian response so we can maintain an inner equilibrium, something so palpably present in sanctified people. When we realize that the aggression of others against us is a reflection of the very same impulse in us—that it is a sign that we have been protected from our own precarious humanity only as a result of God's grace—only then are we provided a rung on the spiritual ladder; only then do we begin to show patience and, ultimately, become grateful for the fact that we are free of those faults. The 11th century Persian theologian, al-Rāghib al-Iṣfahānī (d. CA 443/1060), wrote:

> Keep in mind constantly that any fault you see in another is either manifest in you explicitly or concealed like fire hidden in flint.

This is a disquieting thought but a welcome spiritual insight that, once realized, enables us to see the faults of the oppressor as qualities we ourselves share with him but from which we have been protected. With this insight, we are capable of compassion even for our enemies, because we can see them as permutations of human possibilities inherent in all of us. Then others are seen not just as trials to be endured but also as lessons to be learned, and life becomes a sanctifying path purposefully marked with both malevolent and benevolent milestones that keep us vigilant and spur us on. The Qur'an states, "We have created death and life-after-death to try you and manifest among you those best in deeds" (67:2). Once we gain this insight, we recognize our situation for what it actually is: no more, and no less, than a trial that only seems Kafkaesque to those who have not penetrated its truth yet. And in that recognition resides our liberation.

THE NATURE OF THE OPPRESSED

We are all oppressors, and we are also oppressed. We sometimes oppress ourselves, or we are oppressed at the hands of others or simply by circumstance. A dictionary definition of "oppressed" is "a sense of being weighed down in body or mind," and an oppressed person is in a burdened state of mind that is real. The Qur'an says, "We give no one a burden greater than he can bear" (2:286). Although exegetes differ on the meaning of this verse, many agree it includes the notion that the demands of sacred law are not so onerous that one cannot fulfill them. But it is possible to have earthly challenges that exceed one's capacity to cope.

Less resilient souls will often collapse under stressful conditions, whereas others will face the challenges and overcome them. Various religions and philosophical schools have prescriptive and reconciliatory tenets and advice to help people deal with the inequities and imbalances we find in life. The Hindus attribute the variation in people's states to variations in the state of their Karma; the Abrahamic faiths, on the other hand, see such disparities as provident trials of existence, and as a manifestation of divine wisdom, as well as of our own human failures embedded within them.

The Qur'an directly addresses the issue of social inequities. When some of the Quraysh objected to the Qur'an being revealed to a relatively poor and orphaned man among them, a person with little material prestige despite his aristocratic lineage, the Qur'an refuted them:

> And they said, "Why wasn't this Qur'an revealed to a man of importance from one of the two cities?" Is it they who distribute the mercy of your Lord? It is We who distribute their livelihood among them in the life of this world, and have elevated some of them to ranks over others, that some may employ others as workers. But the mercy of your Lord is better than what they amass. And were it not that humankind would become a single community, We would have provided those who disbelieve in the Benevolent One with roofs of silver for their houses, and stairs for them to climb and doors for their houses, and couches for them to recline, and decoration. Yet all of that is but the stuff of the life of the world; while the hereafter, with your Lord, is for the conscientious. (43:31-35)

According to the Qur'an, the purpose of social stratification is that it creates hierarchy, which then fosters mutuality and interdependence. However, the Arabic word used in the above verse to indicate "to employ" is *sukhriyyā*, which, with slight alteration of the vowel marking, becomes *sikhriyyā*, "to exploit." This subtle change reflects a profound danger inherent in hierarchy: just as *sukhriyyā* can quickly and easily shift to *sikhriyyā*, so, too, can the social order rapidly shift from mutuality and interdependence to abuse and oppression.

This Qur'anic verse also illustrates that the outward displays of wealth and power so eloquently presented—multistoried mansions, roofs of silver, luxurious sofas, and ornamentations—are merely the life of this world, fleeting and filled with uncertainty and trial. The next life, which is the world of true and everlasting prosperity, is open for all—irrespective of wealth or social status—who choose to strive for it in this world with their lives.

This scenario has been used as a pacifying ace in the hands of the elite, and has led to Leftist critiques of religion, which are not easily dismissed. Nonetheless, like the subtle difference between "to employ" and "to exploit," there is a fine, but just as real, distinction between the cynical materialist who sees only darkness, and the spiritualist who views the darkness of this world in the light of the next. The world is not a paradise but was purposefully created to be filled with chaos, distractions, temptations, and trials, if only to engender in the heart of the spiritual agent a desire for peace and quietude. The trials of this world often force us to the door of God to beg for and to seek an opening into the perfect peace of the next. In seeking the next world of true and sustained peace while one is still in this world, one increases the presence of peace in the here-and-now. According to a prophetic tradition, "When the believer initially enters paradise he is compelled to repeat over and over again, 'Peace, peace, peace.'"

Oppression can occur any time if one person has an advantage over another and misuses that advantage to exploit the other. The result is pain, suffering, and hardship for the oppressed. However, the victim can be healed if the wrong is immediately redressed. Justice is never more effective than when it is meted out swiftly. An illustrative example from the blessed Messenger's life is what he did when one of his men, Khālid b. al-Walīd ؓ, tragically killed some tribesmen who had already surrendered to him. Upon hearing the news, the Messenger ﷺ first raised his hands in prayerful gesture and said, "O God, I am innocent of Khālid's wrong." He then dispatched men with blood money for the dead men's clansmen in order to assuage their vengeful resentment, thus thwarting another cycle of violence.

On the other hand, if the injustice is not redressed, if the wrong is not righted, the oppressed person begins to tire from the weight of the load, and sores begin to fester. As the sores fester, the poison spreads throughout the body, and violent fever sets in. Wrath replaces pain as the person attempts to anesthetize his suffering with vengeance. The Arabic word for revenge, *tashaffi*, means literally "to attempt to be healed." Resentment sets in; revenge gets plotted. The oppressed begins to imagine how he can hurt the oppressor, how he can cause his oppressor to feel his pain. We engage in such retributive behavior in our everyday lives, spurred by the oppression we feel from others. We feel hurt and anger, and we plan revenge. It might take the form of giving a spouse the silent treatment for a few days; it might turn into an attack on the property of those who stole from us; it might be unleashing vicious slander against someone who betrayed us; or it might be a suicide bomb against a long-standing and violent aggressor. As the enormity of the wrong increases, so too often does the enormity of the response.

There are times when the oppressed are helpless in righting the wrong or in exacting revenge; they suffer silently, unable to respond to their condition. At such times, the oppressed might slip into denial about the severity of their actual condition. In modern jargon, codependency sets in: an unspoken pact is made between the oppressor and the oppressed, and means are utilized to maintain the integrity of the oppressed so they do not experience cognitive dissonance. This can last a lifetime in the case of an individual; in the case of a community, it can last centuries.

RELIGION'S ROLE IN THE CYCLE OF OPPRESSION

Religion has performed both a pernicious and a profoundly necessary role in the continued cycle of oppression, being a formidable force on the side of both the oppressor and the oppressed. On the one hand, it has often been so successfully co-opted by the oppressor, that even those representing it have come to align themselves more with the wrongdoer than with the wronged. In many societies, religion has been used by the powerful to maintain certain hierarchies and social practices at the expense of the oppressed, causing both the oppressed and those who sympathize with them to be alienated from the religion itself. Secularists relish this sad fact—religion's complicity in historical wrongs—and often underscore it in their attacks on religion. Yet, at best, theirs is a partial and incomplete history of religion. It can be likened to studying the history of a religion's ego and ignoring its soul.

One would conclude from such a perspective that religion is monstrous. But there is another viewpoint.

Any informed perspective must also include the significant contributions of religious believers, acting from religious duty and impulse, in preventing oppression and establishing vehicles for long-lasting social change. For example, in America, a country founded in the late 18th century as a haven for those fleeing from the religious intolerance that beset most of Europe, the clergy often spearheaded the struggle for justice. Nowhere is this more evident than in the abolitionist movement, which, as in England, was driven largely by Unitarian Christians, who not only provided spiritual support for the oppressed but worked actively to change the hearts and minds of those who perpetuated slavery. While religion has often been used as a reactionary and oppressive force, largely due to its misguided alliances with temporal power, it has also bequeathed to us many, if not most, of humanity's loftiest ideals.

Today, however, religion is increasingly seen not as part of the solution but rather as a central part of the problem. And many religious people would concur, though with the caveat that the "problem" is secularity and *other* religions, certainly not their own. But we must acknowledge the glaring and disturbing truth: Religion is central to the problem. Instead of turning us away from religion, that truth should motivate us to assert that religion must *also* be central to the solution. But this is predicated upon a greater understanding of the aims and ends of religion itself.

For if religion is truly to be used to address the very real trials of modern life, which include misguided militancy in the name of religion, adherents must move beyond the platitudes of interfaith dialogue and reach deep, to draw from the ancient waters of prayer, meditation, and introspection. The noise of secularity—and even the noise of religion—has crowded our minds and left us incapable of thoughtful action. But noise is a hallmark of the modern world. In contrast, at the true heart of every religion lies silence, penetrated by illumination: Buddha, the Enlightened One, under the Lote tree; Moses عليه السلام, the prophet, in the Sinai; Jesus عليه السلام, the Messiah, in the desert; and the Prophet Muḥammad ﷺ in the cave of Ḥirā'. The source and power of religion is in its ineffable presence, as well as in the profound state of spiritual quietude that accompanies it, though it is often absent in modern religious adherents. Religious disquietude, and the problems it foments, has led people to seek other sources of silence for enlightenment, or noise for entertainment, that are less troublesome and less self-righteous than religion. Meanwhile, the cycle of oppression spirals on.

BREAKING THE CYCLE

Oppression occurs when we desire that which is not ours. As such, we must first break the cycle within our own hearts: "Surely, God does not change a people until they change what is in themselves" (13:11). The tyrant who lives in the palace is easy to see, the bully on the street corner is in plain sight, but spotting the tyrant within our own souls—the fire concealed in the flint—is far more challenging. It is easy to see ourselves in the shoes of the oppressed and, thus, as the object of empathy. But seeing the tyrant in the mirror, and recognizing in him a reflection of our own state, is an arduous undertaking. The oppressed must first acknowledge that rulers often times reflect the people they rule. The Prophet Muḥammad ﷺ is reported to have said, "As you are, so are the people put over you." Dr. Martin Luther King, Jr., in his "Letter from Birmingham Jail," wrote:

> In any non-violent campaign there are four basic steps: Collection of the facts to determine whether injustice exists; negotiations; self-purification; and direct action.

King's third step—"self-purification"—is rarely discussed, let alone implemented. But it is introspection that enables us to peer within and identify in ourselves the qualities we abhor in others, thereby putting us on the path to purification. If we have unjust rulers, we must ask ourselves whether we are getting the rulers that we deserve: Are we behaving unjustly with our families, our spouses, and our children? Are we displaying the same arbitrary rules in our offices, work places, and homes that we find so abhorrent in our streets and institutions and government? If so, then before we can expect a change in the world, we must first expect one in ourselves. The Qur'an states, "God does not remove a blessing that has been bestowed upon a people until they themselves are ungrateful for it" (8:53). This verse indicates that change occurs in both directions: toward good or toward evil, toward a restorative state or a destructive one. When we become a people of introspection and judge ourselves before we quickly judge those over us, only then will we be able to transform our condition.

Oppression too often engenders in the oppressed overwhelming emotions of sadness, anger, bitterness, and rancor, and leads them to pursue what they perceive as a righteous fight for restitution, which in reality is little more than an expression of vengeful retribution. The Prophet Muḥammad ﷺ, when asked to curse some oppressors, replied, "I was not sent to curse but rather to mercifully guide." This statement reveals precisely the point of this essay: If we are to help others, we cannot wish them ill. In recognizing that the oppressor also needs help, we can see him as a trial from God, and not as an independent agent acting independently of God's providential will.

Cursing or hating or wishing ill upon the oppressor is the antithesis of the prophetic guidance, which calls for mercy.

But here, one must keep in mind the distinction mentioned previously: Mercy toward the oppressor does not preclude resistance to his wrongs, nor does it imply that one should suffer in silence. Rather, it is an inward disposition that allows one to break the very cycles that brought about the wrongs one is attempting to redress. Many of the prophets were warriors in the tradition of spiritual chivalry, who, like David عليه السلام, fought the Goliaths of the world. But they engaged in the struggle knowing that their tribulation was sent by God, and thus they acted accordingly; they were open to the possibility that the enemy could turn into a friend, and they never killed out of revenge or hatred. And while prophets and those who truly follow them—as opposed to those who merely claim to do so—are not immune from feeling anger and desiring retribution, their God-consciousness protects them both from acting upon those impulses and from letting them take root in their hearts.

Whether one is successful in redressing wrongs or meting out justice is less important than whether one strives to do so, acting from compassion. Ultimately, those wrongs not redressed in this world will be righted in the next. Desire for God's forgiveness should be our impetus for forgiving others their wrongs against us. This is eloquently enunciated in the Lord's Prayer: "And forgive us our trespasses, as we forgive those who trespass against us." We cannot expect God to forgive us when we are unwilling to forgive others. Jesus Christ عليه السلام purportedly said:

> Pass no judgment, and you will not be judged. For as you judge, so shall you be judged, and whatever measure you deal out to others will be dealt back to you. Why do you look at the speck of sawdust in your brother's eye with never a thought of the great plank in your own?[1]

This is the true essence of forgiveness: in forgiving others, we are implicitly recognizing that they are reflections of ourselves. Forgive-

---

1 See Matthew 7:1-4.

ness does not imply that we forgo restitution and justice; rather, by looking at our own wrongs, we begin to be less judgmental of others and more able to see ourselves in them. Our desire for collective justice diminishes as our yearning for personal grace increases. Forgiveness and justice are both essential to balance and conviviality in human relations. Paradoxical as it may seem on the surface, both justice and mercy are intrinsic qualities of God. In our own selves the two qualities co-exist, and in tempering one with the other, we are taking upon ourselves an attribute of God. In pursuing either forgiveness or justice, we invite God to reveal Himself to us.

Forgiveness is difficult because it collides with our desire for revenge. When the Bible says, "Vengeance is mine; I will repay, saith the Lord,"[2] it is reminding us of a higher truth, for only with God lies absolute justice, absolute knowledge. To judge a matter without doubt is to claim omniscience. God alone can judge a matter without the possibility of error. Our willingness to forgo our own judgment for a higher judgment allows the space for grace to enter the world. In allowing grace, we are inviting God back into our world, and it is no coincidence that the word in Arabic for "prayer" and the word for "invitation" are one and the same.

THE POWER OF PRAYER

How then do we heal the hearts of those who suffer, with no courts to give them their day, and no advocates to chronicle their grievances and demand they be redressed? We cannot. And we must recognize our own inability to do that; we must weep, not only for them, but more for ourselves, that we are so impotent. For God alone has the power to heal their hearts; God alone has the power to redress their wrongs; and God alone has the power to punish their oppressors. God may do so at the hands of the righteous or at the hands of other oppressors, or God may give them respite until "the day when the

2 See Romans 12:19 and Deuteronomy 32:35.

eyes are turned upside down and hearts are melted into thin air," but redress God will.

Imam al-Darʿī wrote his *Prayer of the Oppressed* for the forsaken people, for the helpless who have no advocate, no defender, no guardian but God, because he knew the secret of utter helplessness: it is the human condition. He begins his poem with the plea:

> O You, Whose mercy is a refuge for all those
> In dire need who flee to You to lose their woes

Power, other than God's, is an illusion, and those who are empowered by God are often deluded into using that power in pursuit of their own desires. The prayer of the oppressed is the prayer of those who have no resistance left in them, those who cannot rely on themselves anymore because they are worn out and weary. This is the prayer of the early Muslims of Mecca. It is not a prayer that supplicates for the destruction of one's enemies; it asks only that their oppression be thwarted and repelled. There is no better exemplar of this than the blessed Prophet Muḥammad ﷺ. After being abused and driven out of Taif, he prayed:

> O Lord, to You alone I complain of my diminished strength, limited strategy, and insignificance in the eyes of others. Most Merciful of those who show mercy, You are Lord of the downtrodden and my Lord: to whom will You leave me? To those who mistreat me, or to an enemy in whose hands You place my affair? As long as Your wrath is not upon me, it concerns me not, although security is easier for me. I seek refuge in the light of Your Countenance, which illuminates darkness; and the affair of this world and the next is set right from Your wrath descending upon me, or Your displeasure enveloping me. For You alone have the right to reprimand until You are pleased; and there is no strength, no power, save with You.

The tyrant's greatest strength is the fear he instills in others, but prayer is the antidote to that fear. So what happens when people are free of that fear? What happens when, as the Qur'an states, "Those who are told, 'People are gathering to harm you' are increased in faith and cry, 'God suffices us and He is the best of protectors'" (3:173)? When people are free of the fear of false deities, whether those deities are rank, position, power, wealth, fame, glory, or fear itself, none can command and control them except the object of their devotion. And, for Muslims, the perfected embodiment of this freedom, the one absolutely free from both the worship and the fear of false deities, is the blessed Prophet Muḥammad ﷺ.

For the first thirteen years of his mission, the Prophet Muḥammad ﷺ was tyrannized and ostracized by his own people; yet he did not feel humiliated, because he never viewed them as oppressors. Instead, he saw the Hand of God working through them in their attempt to abase him; and thus they succeeded only in elevating him in God's gaze. What the people saw was the orphan of the clan of Hāshim with no apparent protector or guardian. So certain were they of this that they sent their children and their slaves to attack him and chase him out. The Prophet ﷺ then turned to God in total servitude with the helplessness of one who knows he has God alone to turn to; whereupon two angels descended from the heavens and offered to destroy the village upon his command. But the Prophet ﷺ did not desire destruction, because he was not consumed with hatred or vengeance; instead, he felt compassion for his oppressors. While he acknowledged the wrongs of the world, metaphysically he saw no wrongs, but only the deeper reality of divine purpose, the vast plan of God in all its mysterious majesty. The Prophet Muḥammad ﷺ could only see God, and the shadows of this world disappeared in the presence of that dazzling light. So, instead of asking for their destruction, he prayed for their guidance and salvation. Five times a day, the Prophet Muḥammad ﷺ prayed:

> O God! You are light, and from You is light. Place light in my heart and on my tongue and in my eyes and in my ears and in front of me and to the right of me and to the left of me and behind me and in my presence. Place light in my nerves and in my bones and in my flesh. Make me live in light; grant me light; give me light; make me light.

If one lives in light, one does not obsess about the shadows. Oppression exists; but we act heedlessly if we empower it and animate it with a life it should never be granted. If, instead, we place wrongs where they belong, in the field of God's testing ground, we are able to distance ourselves—and our hearts—from them. In these wrongs, we then recognize the obstacles in our own path to Him, as well as obstacles for the oppressors, preventing them from moving nearer unto God. So when wrongs and injustices become too large for us to remove, as is often the case, then we must turn to the One who placed them in our path and call upon Him for assistance. This is precisely the purpose of Imam al-Darʿī's invocation.

The invocation takes us back to the elemental and the essential: supplicating, invoking, pleading, imploring, and ultimately begging God to remove us from harm's way. It is saying, "Let harm be as it may, but remove it from our way. It is Your creation, here with Your permission, always of the Earth and destined to be as long as we exist and the Earth is with us; but You alone allow it, and You alone can protect us from it." In calling on God in this way, the secret of injustice is revealed to us: it exists to strengthen our faith, to bring us closer to God. Herein lies the irony of ironies: from Him, to Him, and for Him is the stuff of our souls, and until we realize that fully in our entire being, the world will continue to brutalize us. Its gruesome nature will continue to overwhelm and confound us until we see it for what it is: a shadow, present only because of the absence of His light in our hearts. The Qur'an illustrates this point succinctly in this verse: "And [God relented] to the three left behind, so that the earth seemed too small for them for all its spaciousness, and their own souls beleaguered them, and they thought there was no refuge from God except to God; then God relented toward them, that they might repent. For God is forgiving, merciful" (9:118). The refuge is from God to God. God is the source of all of our trials and tribulations, and we can either hate God for it, as some have chosen, or painfully recognize that the secret of all of our troubles is in fleeing to God from God.

The moment we let the light of God into our hearts, the moment those shadows are dispelled, then we can return to our true selves and act with ease and affability. Our enemies will no longer be our enemies but potential friends. "Perhaps God will place love between you and those you now hold as enemies, and God is Omnipotent, and God is Oft-Forgiving, Merciful," as the Qur'an so eloquently states (60:7). The people causing us to suffer are seen for what they are: people who are, themselves, suffering. They are to be empathized with, not envied. Those who are truly worthy of envy are not those with temporal power. Rather, they are the powerless who, in their powerlessness, move nearer to God because they realize their absolute dependence upon God alone. Such "powerless" people are the ones given true power and freedom by God.

THE GIFT OF POWERLESSNESS

Most of the Muslim world is now experiencing a state of powerlessness, and therein lies a great opportunity. The loss of state power, military might, sovereignty, and control is not the end of Islam but a new beginning. It may be the end of political Islam, but it surely portends the resurgence of spiritual Islam. The Prophet Muḥammad ﷺ said, "Islam began as an alien thing, and it will return as an alien thing, so blessed are the strangers."

"Who are the strangers?" he was asked.

"They are those who rectify my path after people have corrupted it."

When Islam was first taught in Mecca, the people there saw it as a radical innovation, a severe threat to their way of life, which they believed was superior to Islam. Islam was indeed "an alien thing" since the extant culture included, among other practices, burying daughters alive, subjugating women, exploiting the poor with usury, enslaving defenseless people, and warring against an entire tribe based on collective guilt over the actions of one of its members. It was a hierarchical and unjust place where some people were considered superior to others based upon their lineage and complexion. Initially the Prophet ﷺ was persecuted for teaching that women were not chattel but had rights, that slavery was immoral, and that people in indentured bondage should be liberated. He taught that feeding the hungry and the homeless was one of the greatest acts of charity one could perform, and he himself fed, on average, seventy homeless people each day. He affirmed that dignity lay in piety and self-control, while degradation was in moral incontinence and self-abandonment. He prohibited domestic violence, child abuse, and economic exploitation of the poor, and he was the first in human history to declare that all people are created equal and that the color of their skin, their gender, or their beliefs did not outweigh that equality before God, as the only thing that raised one person above another was conscientiousness.[3]

Even though the Prophet Muḥammad ﷺ was powerless for the first thirteen years of his mission, he never prayed against his oppressors, who included his own kinsmen. He never carried out punitive measures against them, nor did he organize subversive groups to undermine the peace and security of society. He was patient and forbearing, and he continued to call others to the way of his Lord with wisdom and beautiful exhortation. He also sent some of his followers to live in the Christian land of Negus in East Africa, counseling them to follow the laws and not to undermine state authority or abuse their host's generosity.

---

3 The word *taqwā* is used in the Qur'anic verse, "Surely the most dignified of you in God's view are the most in *taqwā*" (49:13). *Taqwā* is a difficult word to translate. Its root meaning is "to ward off harm." The closest word in English is probably "piety," which is from a Latin word, *pietās*, meaning "dutiful conduct." This idea is found in the Greek concept *arête*, "acting according to one's virtue or with excellence." "Piety," however, has fallen on hard times and is considered quaint, even ridiculed. "Conscientiousness" is from a Latin root, which originally meant "to know right from wrong" and in English means "the state of recognizing the difference between right and wrong with regard to one's conduct, coupled with a sense that one should act accordingly." This is close to the meaning of *taqwā* in Arabic, with the exception that the English word is more subjective, whereas *taqwā* in Islamic tradition relates to conformity with sacred law. Hence, one becomes more dignified as one increases in moral conduct and acts according to the dictates of one's conscience that is informed by revelation.

The Prophet ﷺ was subject to oppression while in Mecca, and his clan was denied food and aid and left to starve—an all-too-common phenomenon in modern times, when sanctions levied against countries cause starvation and death among the population. During this period, when the Prophet ﷺ and his family ate tree leaves and barely eked out a living in the barren wilderness in and around Mecca, his faith and trust in God never wavered. This enabled him to live without hatred or rancor toward his oppressors. On the contrary, when a woman fell ill who used to put thorns in his path every morning to irk him, he visited her home to inquire about her health and to wish her well. In subsequent years, when he gained ascendancy and power over his enemies, he showed much magnanimity and forgave them for their wrongs, with the exception of four men whose "crimes against humanity," to use a contemporary term, were so heinous that they could not be forgotten or forgiven. Such exceptional crimes are certainly committed today, but we would do well to remind ourselves that the essential truth of overcoming hatred, anger, and resentment is at the core of our Prophet's teaching.

That such principles may seem extrinsic to many Muslims today is in accordance with the Prophet's prediction that his teachings would be alien to even its own adherents. Unfortunately, in a case of historical repetition, what is understood as Islam today in some circles harks back to tribal Islam, in which *Banī Islām* is pitted against *Banī Kufr*, and in which all of a tribe's people are guilty of the actions of a few. But despite the zealous militancy of a few misguided fools who believe they are defending the honor of Muslims, this is a time to recognize the gift of utter helplessness, and a golden opportunity for Muslims to re-learn the sunnah of the oppressed taught by the Prophet Muḥammad ﷺ while he was in Mecca.

Far from being abrogated when things are going well, the Qur'anic verses revealed in Mecca—those that encourage turning the other cheek and forgiving those who do wrong—are meant to inculcate qualities that are essential to Muslims when they are empowered. But without learning this sunnah, they are not worthy of being empowered, as they are likely to continue the cycle of oppression. For unlike Ṣalāḥ al-Dīn (d.589/1193), who could march into Jerusalem and not exact revenge but display the same magnanimity and mercy his exemplar did in Mecca, unlearned and undisciplined souls in the same situation would exact revenge and, in doing so, soil the reputation of Muslims and Islam for all time. Wilfrid Scawen Blunt (d. 1922), the Arabist who opposed British imperial pursuits in the Muslim world and who was imprisoned for his support of the Irish opposition to England, well understood the high price of sovereign and temporal power to the religion of Islam. In his 1882 book, *The Future of Islam*, he wrote:

> One great result the fall of Constantinople certainly will have, which I believe will be a beneficial one. It will give to ... [Islam] a more distinctly religious character than it has for many centuries possessed, and by forcing believers to depend upon spiritual instead of temporal arms will restore to them, more than any political victories could do, their lost moral life. Even independently of considerations of race as between Turk and Arab, I believe that the fall of the Muslim Empire, as a great temporal dominion, would relieve Islam of a burden of sovereignty which she is no longer able in the face of the modern world to support. She would escape the stigma of political depravity now clinging to her, and her aims would be simplified and intensified.... I do not, therefore, see in territorial losses a sign of Islam's ruin as a moral and intellectual force in the world."[4]

Blunt was a learned man, with knowledge and experience of the Muslim world of the time; he was not only a supporter of Ahmed Urabi (d. 1911) and the Urabi Revolt of 1879 in Egypt against the British, but a lover of all things Arab and Muslim. He also had first hand experience and knowledge of the levels of corruption to be encountered at all strata of Muslim society.

Blunt's insightful observation—that "territorial losses" do not signal "Islam's ruin as a moral and intellectual force"—is especially relevant today. For too long, Muslims have ignored the dire need, not

4 Wilfrid Scawen Blunt, *The Future of Islam* (London: Routledge Curzon, 2002), 53.

for political revival, but for a spiritual and moral renaissance in the Muslim world. When Muslims nowadays clamor for Islamic governance, they are more often than not asking for more just government. The strongest Muslim spiritual movement in the world today is arguably in Turkey, which happens to have the most secularized government in the Muslim world. Conversely, the Muslim countries that claim to have Islamic governance happen to be the most corrupt countries in the Muslim world. The least corrupt governments in the world today are the most secular; the Scandinavian countries, for instance, have the most social justice and are consistently ranked lowest on the corruption indexes. Meanwhile, the highest rankings tend to include Muslim governments and peoples.

The Prophet Muḥammad ﷺ said, "The Qur'an and government (*sulṭān*) will soon part ways, so go where the Qur'an goes, and abandon the government." According to an absolutely sound hadith, the Prophet ﷺ stated, "Islamic governance will follow the prophetic pattern for thirty years; after that, it will become monarchies that adhere to it with violence; then, it will become tyrannies; and finally it will be restored to a government upon the pattern of prophets." This last phase, according to all the great hadith commentators, is near the end of time, with the advent of the Mahdi.

The modern Muslim obsession with so-called Islamic governance is a dangerous fantasy. It has led to a politicization of Islam that has eviscerated its spiritual power and exalted indiscriminate violence as a "justifiable means" to Islamic ends. When suicide bombers first emerged in the Muslim world, borrowing a page from Marxist-influenced Hindu political movements of Southeast Asia, traditional scholars condemned the innovation. But soon, extremist Muslims began quoting Qur'anic verses and hadith to support violent measures as a legitimate response to intolerable social conditions and oppression. As popular support for this innovation gained ground in Palestine and Lebanon, the scholars were drowned out, and before long, even the Arabic news media adopted references to "martyrdom operations."

Now we get daily reports of innocent people, mostly Muslim, being killed in Iraq, Pakistan, Afghanistan, and even in America and Great Britain; meanwhile the scholars begin to sound hollow as they attempt to draw a distinction between legitimate and illegitimate uses of violence. The tragic state of Muslims embroiled in oppression—economic and militaristic—has naturally caused many to lose their quietude and equilibrium. It is hard to sit in judgment of people in the Gaza Strip or Afghanistan, who are driven to violence by the inhumane and oppressive conditions they live under; the rest of us, however, have no excuse for succumbing to reactive feelings and advocating violent counter-measures that deny the aggressors' humanity.

Until Muslims learn and internalize the sunnah of powerlessness, we will not be worthy of assuming the responsibility that comes with power, and for God to give it to us before we are ready and prepared would be an abandonment of His providence for this community. Our Prophet ﷺ stated, "This ummah is one that God has shown mercy to; its purging will be in this world with civil strife, earthquakes, and calamities." He ﷺ also stunningly prophesied that, "The time is coming soon when the nations of this world will consume your resources as diners consume the food on their plate."

The companions asked, "Is it because of our weakness in numbers?"

To this, he ﷺ replied, "Not at all; you are multitudes, but you are inconsequential, like the froth and flotsam created by the violent current of a water flow. The awe that your enemies previously held you in will be lost, and debilitation with be thrust into your hearts."

"What is the debilitation, O Messenger of God?" they asked.

"Love of materialism, and a disdain for struggle," replied the Prophet ﷺ.

What is important to glean from this hadith is that the companions did not ask what made the oppressor strong, but what made the oppressed weak. However, the Prophet ﷺ did not answer them at the logistical level of numbers and tactics, but instead elevated them to see the spiritual reality behind an oppressed people's weakness. It is ultimately in the state of our hearts that our weakness resides, as we lose our spiritual anchoring and are set adrift in a storm of materialism and self-indulgence.

Only through introspection, through a critical inward look at our emotional and mental states, can we begin the process of healing our hearts. "And We revealed the Qur'an to be a healing for [the hearts]" (17:82). A true moral and spiritual renaissance can only occur among Muslims if and when they grasp and acknowledge the radical premises of the Qur'an, especially its entirely self-critical approach to the human condition. The Qur'an is a book that forces one to examine and change one's own condition before questioning or demanding change in anyone or any condition outside oneself. The Qur'an does not let up until its profound conclusion is understood: that God is the lord of humanity, the sovereign of humanity, and the god of humanity, and that we will continue to suffer from unrelenting whisperings in our hearts as long as we are turned away from our one true lord, sovereign, and god (114:1-6).

The devil's game is the blame game, and those enticed by it will end up playing with him in Hell. As the Qur'an states: "And Satan will say when the matter is decided, 'God actually pledged you the true promise; I also made you a promise, but I betrayed you. I had no authority over you, except that I invited you and you responded to me. So do not blame me, but blame yourselves. I am not your savior, and you are not my savior. I repudiate your previous association of me with God; for the wrongdoers there is painful punishment'" (14:22). The instigator of the blame game finally owns up and tells his followers, who played it so well in this world, that they have only themselves to blame. In an extraordinarily profound explication of the nature of blame, we find in another verse:

> God will say, "Enter the Fire, in the company of communities of sprites and humans who passed away before you." Every time a people enters, it

> curses another of its kind, until they have all followed along into Hellfire. The last of them will say of the first, "Our Lord, they deluded us, so give them double the penalty of Fire." God will say, "Double for everyone!" But you do not know. And the first of them will say to the last of them, "You have no advantage over us now, so taste the torment for what you used to do" (7:38-39).

Immediately after, the Qur'an describes the state of the people of Paradise: "As for those who believe and do good works, We do not burden a soul beyond its capacity. They are the inhabitants of the Garden where they will abide. And We will remove rancor from their hearts" (7:42). The people of Hell live there as they lived here, cursing others for their troubles and asking that the others be punished more harshly than them, which results in their prayer's being answered against themselves as well.

On the other hand, the people of Paradise were engaged in good deeds here; and while some may have died without fully purifying their hearts of rancor, it is removed from them in that perfect abode, wherein they abide as brothers and sisters, free of fault. Our time here on earth allows us to work on our souls and purify our hearts in preparation for that great Day of Judgment. For indeed, it is a day where "neither wealth nor children will avail; only the one who brings to God a heart free of rancor will have benefit" (26:88-89). Muslims should resist the temptation to blame others and should look into our own hearts and begin the process of purification. Until we change first in our selves what we desire to see changed in the world, nothing else will change. "For surely, God does not change a people's condition until they change what is in themselves" (13:11).

In these troubled times, rife with oppression, many Muslims have been praying for God's victory over their enemies, and those prayers seem to go unanswered. What many do not grasp, however, is that the One called upon is merciful, and so He will not grant to those He loves a victory over their enemies if in that material victory is their spiritual defeat. Truly, it is better to be oppressed than to be an oppressor. Only those who are ready to break the cycle of oppression—who struggle solely for the sake of God and desire their hearts to be healed—are spiritually prepared for victory. For if God grants you victory and you are not prepared for it, you may find yourself in the position of the one you despised. And the vicious cycle of hatred and oppression will continue. So let us all pray for victory, not just over the enemy out there, but also over the enemy within.

A Reflection on Divine Love

MANY MUSLIMS BELIEVE that the idea, "God loves everyone," is simply wrong and incongruous with Islamic teachings. Verses abound in the Qur'an decrying those God does not love: liars, hypocrites, oppressors, the arrogant, boastful braggarts, and those who love praise for that which they have not done, among others. Reading these verses, it is easy to begin to resent such people and to believe that God does not love *everyone*. However, if we look closely at these people, we see elements of ourselves in them.

What is true of any man is true of all men; the only difference is in the degree to which it is true. Prophets and sanctified saints are the only exceptions to this universal truth. Jesus ﷺ states, as recorded in *al-Muwaṭṭā'* of Imam Mālik (d. 179/795):

> Do not, like lords, look upon the faults of others. Rather, like servants, look after your own faults. In truth, humanity is comprised of only two types of people: the afflicted and the sound. So show mercy to the afflicted, and praise God for well-being.

It is never the sinner that one should hate, but only the sin; for the essence of all humanity is a soul created in submission to its Creator. Whether that soul acknowledges this on a conscious level or not is a matter of grace, and this understanding enables us to look at others with compassion. All people, everywhere and throughout time, suffer great tribulation at various points in their lives. At this very moment, hearts are breaking and lives are being shattered, women abused, children violated, and people dying while their loved ones are crying. Also at this very moment, other hearts are rejoicing, babies are being born, mothers are nurturing, smiles are given freely, charity is being distributed, and lovers are uniting. The airport is one of the great metaphors of our time: sad, happy, and indifferent faces are all to be seen there, as people part with loved ones, greet their beloveds, or simply wait to pick up or let off people they barely know. Sad, happy, and indifferent are the states that sum up our collective body of souls. In the next life, however, there is only bliss or wretchedness, joy or sorrow—no indifference.

According to a beautiful hadith, the Prophet ﷺ said that on the Last Day, when the last two souls are brought forth before God, they are both condemned to hell. As the angels escort them to their final fiery abode, one of them wistfully looks back. Thereupon, God commands the angels to bring him back and asks the man why he turned back. The man replies, "I was expecting something else from You." God responds, commanding the angels, "Take him to My Garden."

It is our expectation of God that determines where we are. This points up the need for thinking well not only of God but also of God's creation, despite the fact that we are all messy, imperfect works in progress, struggling along in this journey.

We either surrender to God or to the substitutes for God, which are invariably hollow. But true love, which is the love of God, is the single most powerful force in the world. It is a love that "alters not when it alteration finds." It grows and never diminishes. If someone claims to have lost it, it can only be said that such a person did not have it to begin with. "It is the star to every wandering bark." And in loving God, one must paradoxically love all of God's creation, merely for the incontrovertible fact that everything *is* God's creation. God *does* love everything in that He brought everything into existence from an act of divine love, and those who love God purely, and with the penetrating inner eye of reality, can only be a mercy while in the world. This does not mean that we love the evil that emanates from moral agents. In fact, it is an act of faith to loathe what is loathsome to God. So when God says He does not love oppressors, it is their oppression that we must loath. In denying the humanity that is inherent in the oppressor, we miss the point and disallow the possibility that the door of God's mercy and love is open to everyone. If we truly believe that we love for everyone what we love for ourselves, then we should want everyone, no matter their state of being or their station in life, to enter that door of God's mercy and love, through repentance and contrition. Allowing for this possibility enables us to be a mercy, as the Prophet 🕊 was.

What follows is a profound explication of this truth by Emir ʿAbd al-Qādir al-Jazāʾirī (d. 1300/1883), perhaps the last exemplar of Islam on all the levels of prophetic character—as a teacher, warrior, statesman, father, and fully awakened master of the path of the prophets:

> "They love God, and God loves them" (5:54). You should know that the love the Real has for creation is of various kinds. One type is the divine love for them before they came into existence; and another is the divine love after they were created. These two types are further categorized into two other types: one is the divine love of the elect, and the other is the divine love of the elite of the elect. As for the first [the divine love before creation], it permeates all of existence, despite the varieties of types, kinds, and characters. It is understood in the famous dictum known well to the folk of spirit,[1] "I was a hidden treasure who loved to be known, so I created this creation to introduce Myself, and through it, they came to know Me." This love is the love that brought the world into existence: "I created humankind and sprites only to adore Me" (51:56). In other words, "to know Me." This is the very love we have mentioned; it is God's inclination to manifest His divine names and attributes, and this is an inclination of the essential divine nature, which is not colored with a name or an attribute, because the names do not manifest at this level of consideration.[2] Then, this inclination of divine love for self-

---

[1] The word used in Arabic is *qawm*, which literally means "folk". However, in the technical vocabulary of *taṣawwuf* (Sufism), it refers to the Sufis themselves. This is based upon the famous hadith in which the angels tell God of a group of people remembering Him, and they mention one who was not a participant but was only sitting in their company. To this God replies, "*humu l-qawmu lā yashqā bihim jalīsuhum*," meaning, "They are a folk (*qawm*) with whom even the one sitting is saved," simply due to his being in their company. While the word "folk" is now considered archaic, it is still in use; and given that it means both "men" and "people" and originally meant "an army," "folk" seems most appropriate as a translation of *qawm*, given that *qawm* in classical Arabic refers specifically to men-folk.

[2] In classical Muslim theology, an attribute (*ṣifah*) or a substantive name (*ism*) of God is neither the essence of God nor other than the essence. This means that no attribute or

expression extended itself through all of the divine names and sought to manifest through the epiphanies of the divine traces as they had been previously hidden in the divine essence, consumed in the divine unity. But once God created them, they knew God as God desired to be known, given that the divine will is unassailable. Every type of creature knew God based upon the level of understanding and preparedness that God had bestowed upon it. As for the angels, each one is a type unto itself, and each has a station and rank, just as all the rest of creation has types and ranks. None can either relinquish or surpass its rank, and their acceptance is predicated upon the degree of knowledge of God that they have. For without a doubt, they increased in their knowledge when Adam ﷺ taught them the names, as the Exalted has taught us in the Qur'an. As for inanimate objects, beasts, and animals other than humans, they have a natural disposition that entails a divine knowledge that neither increases nor decreases. Each of them also has a station, and it cannot exceed its boundaries of knowledge. As for the human being, he or she has a primordial knowledge that [although lost upon entering the world] can undergo a *renovatio*.[3] Its renovation is based upon the condition of his or her outward state; I mean by this the state of the soul and intellect.[4] For in reality, all of knowledge is concentrated in the individual's reality; it simply manifests from one time to another, based upon the divine will, because the human reality is contained in each person. And each human being, in that he or she is a human being, is open to the possibility of the rank of "perfected human." However, they will vary in the way their human perfection manifests itself in them.

As for the first type of divine love, which is that of the elect, this is reserved for only certain ones among God's servants. Examples of this are found in the Qur'an: "Surely God loves those who repent" (2:222). Also included among those God loves are those who purify themselves, the patient, the grateful, those who place their trust in God, those "who fight

---

name can contain a summation of God that only God's essence contains.

3 *Renovatio* is a Latin theological term that seems to convey perfectly the Arabic *tajdīd*, "renewal". In classical Christian theology, the corrupted *imago dei* (image of God) is restored to its original integrity. This conveys well the meaning intended here, and God knows best.

4 "Intellect" here refers to the medieval understanding of intellect, which differed from reason. Intellect was the function of one's intelligence that distinguished between the real and the apparent—hence the Latin, *intellectus* (= *inte[r] lectus*), to distinguish between or to judge between (the real and the false).

> in ranks for the sake of God" (61:4), not to mention all the other beloveds God mentions in the Qur'an who have embodied certain qualities and characteristics that necessitate this special love from the Real, Exalted God. Nonetheless, it is a type of love that veils and [yet] allows for a transcendent understanding of God. Moreover, it is a love that is unobtainable for certain types of people, as mentioned in the verses, "God loves not oppressors," (3:57), and "God loves not those who cover truth with lies" (3:32). Despite that, they are still enveloped in the first type of divine love [that is, divine love before they came into existence].
>
> As for the second type of special divine love, it is for the elect of the elite; it is indicated in the sacred hadith,[5] "My servant continues to draw near unto Me through voluntary acts of devotion until I love him. And when I love him, I become the hearing with which he hears, the sight with which he sees, the hand with which he strikes, and the foot with which he walks. Were he to ask something of Me, I would assuredly grant it; were he to seek refuge in Me, I would grant it."[6] In other words, the identity of the Real is revealed to him as the secret of his own outward and inward faculties. This type of divine love occurs with an epiphany upon the beloved, the fruit of which is manifest in this world due to the divine witnessing and vision that occurs in the imaginal[7] realm; or it occurs with other things also, as an effusion of experiential knowledge through myriad gifts. As for the previous special type of love, it is still a veiled love, given that its possessor is still trapped in the illusion of otherness and duality. Hence, its fruits only manifest in the next world. For this reason, ʿAṭā' Allāh (d.709/1309) says in his *Aphorisms* (*al-Ḥikam*), "The devoted servants and detached ones leave this world while their hearts are still filled with otherness."[8]

This last love is attained only by those who possess the direct knowledge of God described in the sacred hadith above. Furthermore, it is only attained by one who has in his or her heart that universal love for

---

5 A sacred hadith (*ḥadīth qudsī*) neither holds the rank of a hadith, which is a statement from the Prophet ﷺ, nor of the Qur'an. It holds a third rank, which is a divine statement; i.e., it is considered revelation, but unlike the Qur'an, it is uttered in the words of the Prophet Muḥammad ﷺ; we could say it is the Prophet ﷺ paraphrasing his Lord.

6 This hadith is recorded by Imam al-Bukhārī and is considered absolutely true.

7 The emir uses the expression *ʿalā takhyīl*, which is related to imagination but is not to be confused with the modern usage of this word; hence, *imaginal*.

8 Emir ʿAbd al-Qādir al-Jazā'irī, *al-Mawāqif*, vol. 1 (Beirut: Dār al-Kutub al-ʿIlmiyyah, 2004), 196-197, *mawqif* no. 105.

all of creation that is understood in the verse, "My Mercy encompasses all things" (7:156). It is the mercy that the Messenger of God ﷺ spoke of when he said, "You will not truly believe until you show mercy to one another."

To this, a companion responded, "But Messenger of God, all of us show mercy to others."

The Prophet ﷺ explained, "I am not speaking of the mercy one of you shows to his friend but of universal mercy—mercy to all of humanity."

Regarding the famous hadith, "None of you truly believes until he loves for his brother what he loves for himself," Imam al-Nawawī (d. 676/1277) states in his commentary that this love includes all of humanity. He further elucidates that it is a love that goes against our very nature; it is angelic in nature, and it is only obtained by negating the ego.

This struggle with the ego—with our own vengeful soul—is one of the most difficult challenges we face. But in succeeding in this struggle, we are not only able to forgive: we are also able to strike, when the only appropriate response is a strike—but with the Hand of God, not with the hand of our own ego because it is an undeniable reality of the world that miscreants exist, that there are human demons whose evil must be thwarted. This is the essence of jihad: to take up the sword in order to remove the sword from the hands of those who wish to do evil in the world. However, the mujahid must be purified from his own ego so he can act as an agent of the divine in the world. This was the reality of the Prophet ﷺ on the battlefield, about whom God said, "And when you threw, you did not throw, but rather God threw" (8:17). It is only such people who are worthy of being the caliphs of God upon the earth. They are the ones God will empower to rule. And for those who do not possess these qualities but still have the love of God, God's greatest gift is to leave them powerless. God's privation is itself a gift, for He withholds not from want but from wisdom.

About the Author

IMAM MUḤAMMAD B. MUḤAMMAD b. Aḥmad b. Nāṣir al-Darʿī (d. 1085/1674) was born to a humble family in a small village in southern Morocco, but went on to become a giant among the luminaries of Islam. He was a master of several Islamic sciences, founded a spiritual center, was a prolific author, memorized many books, texts, and poems, and perhaps most consequential of all, authored this extraordinary invocation. He may have been materially poor, but he spiritually enriched—and continues to enrich—untold numbers of Muslims worldwide.

Imam al-Darʿī grew up in destitute conditions in Tamegroute, a remote village in the valley of the Draa River, in the vicinity of Sijilmasa, a Moroccan city known for its learning, spirituality, and prodigious output of mystics and scholars. Living during the most difficult and turbulent time in Morocco's Muslim history, he witnessed the general decline of Muslim power and the rapid rise of European naval strength and subsequent colonial ambitions.

The year of Imam al-Darʿī's birth, 1012/1603, also marks the death of one of the most extraordinary monarchs in Morocco's history, Sultan Ahmad al-Mansour al-Dhahabi, "the Golden One," under whose intelligent and enlightened rule the country had prospered at home and maintained good relations abroad (with one notable exception).[1] In fact, in 1011/1602, the sultan invited Queen Elizabeth I (d. 1012/1603) of Great Britain to enter into an alliance with him to jointly invade America, freeing it from Spanish dominion. In his letter to the Queen,

1 The exception is the military mission he sent to West Africa in 1590. This egregious misadventure, including the criminal capture of Mali's capital Timbuktu, is a great and perhaps irredeemable blemish on his otherwise extraordinary reign. One can only wonder if the chaos that ensued in Morocco, leading to over seventy years of civil strife and insecurity, was not in answer to the prayers of the oppressed Malians, including those of the great scholar Ahmad Baba, who wrote of his city's destruction and his own enslavement at the hands of the Moroccan forces.

the sultan wrote, "With the success from God, our two countries can rule the Americas in peace." His untimely death in 1603, however, led to a civil war that further weakened the country and lasted for more than seventy years.

Despite being born into toilsome times and straitened circumstances, Imam al-Darʿī lived in a relatively safe region. He spent his early childhood devoted to the serious study of the subjects then available to most Moroccan children of his village, such as Qur'anic memorization and orthography, Arabic grammar, and basic Islamic jurisprudence. From a young age, he demonstrated unusual intelligence and a thirst for knowledge that impressed all around him. Despite his poverty, he was known to collect books and to spend what money he had in their acquisition. When he simply could not afford to purchase a book, he would copy it out by hand. Eventually, his library was full of volumes that he himself had copied, complete with his own corrections and extensive annotations.

In a family too poor to afford a bed for him, Imam al-Darʿī slept on the floor. When one of his teachers kindly purchased a mattress for him, he placed his books upon it rather than sleep on it. Later, however, Imam al-Darʿī became a man of means and twice fulfilled the obligation of the sacred pilgrimage, traveling from Morocco to Mecca, the first time in 1070/1660. During his travels, he studied with scholars in the sacred precincts of Mecca and Medina, as well as at al-Azhar University in Egypt. Upon his return to Morocco, he founded a spiritual center, known as a *zāwiyyah*, and had many disciples, as well as students of shariah and the ancillary sciences of Islam.

In the prime of his life, Imam al-Darʿī became a prolific author, producing several scholarly works, including a book of legal opinions, simply entitled *al-Fatāwah;* a biographical work, *al-Fihrisah*, in which he provides short biographies of his teachers; a didactic poem of Mālikī jurisprudence; and books on grammar, the rites of Hajj, and medicine. He also wrote commentaries on several famous works, including a book on sacred timekeeping and astronomy by Abī Muqraʿ (d. 719/1319); Khalīl b. Isḥāq's (d. 767/1366) abridgment of Mālikī law, in which Imam al-Darʿī focuses on the section dealing with inheritance laws; the hadith collections of al-Bukhārī and Muslim; and the famous and widely used didactic poem on morphology, known as *Lāmiyāt al-afʿāl*. Besides his written works, Imam al-Darʿī was also known to have memorized many books, texts, and poems, including the extensive *Tashīl* and the voluminous dictionary *al-Qāmūs*.

The Moroccan historian of the 18th century, Muḥammad al-Ṣaghīr (d. 1160/1747), says about him:

> He was known as Ibn Nāṣir after his grandfather. Imam al-Yūsī [d. 1102/1691] mentions in his compendium of scholars, "He was a master of several Islamic sciences including jurisprudence, Arabic, theology, Qur'anic commentary, hadith and its related subjects, and Sufism. In addition to his deeply-dyed devotion and eschewal of the world, he was fastidiously upright and scrupulous concerning his affairs. He lacked any desire for this world and was a gnostic master who drank from the spring of reality. In spite of his deep knowledge of the inward sciences and his preoccupation with matters of the heart, he was also firmly rooted in outward knowledge, teaching it, as well as writing useful books relating to it. Through him and his knowledge, God benefited many, including seekers of the spiritual path as well as students of religious knowledge. He spent his life teaching his students and spiritually guiding his disciples on the stations of the path. His spiritual state was one of sound outward knowledge, high aspiration, a pleasing nature, and a piercing inner vision, to such a degree that if he spoke or even sighed in the presence of others, his words and his breaths penetrated their hearts."
>
> Al-Yūsī says, "I was one of ten students on a journey with him. We would gather, and, as is the nature of such gatherings, we would indulge in empty talk and carry on. When we parted, he said to me, 'Try and avoid the company of people as much as possible.' When I reached the *Bakriyyah Zāwiyyah*, I married a woman and left the company of such men [as Imam al-Darʿī] and engaged in worldly pursuits for a time, being involved in the affairs of family. After a while, I returned and visited him, and he said to me, 'You should struggle with your ego and your appetites more.'

He began to look at me as if he were saying, 'You did such and such, and you did such and such.' I suddenly felt an overwhelming sense of shame. He then told me that his own teacher used to say, 'If any of you finds himself desiring water, let him wait a little—not because there is any harm in drinking water, but simply to discipline the ego and not accustom it to getting what it desires quickly.' These words left an indelible mark upon my thoughts. Through his insight and unveilings[2] he gave me two basic cures for my disease without confronting me with the specifics of my ailments or exposing my faults. Rather, he limited himself to the necessary, and counseled me with exactly what I needed to treat myself."

In his *Gift of the Friends*, Abū Salīm says [about Imam al-Darīʿ], "He was very exacting in his adherence to the prophetic way, even in his clothing and victuals. He adhered vigilantly to the practice of the Prophet ﷺ in acts of devotion and wont. In that, he conformed to the books of Shaykh al-Marjānī, Ibn Abī Jamrāh, and Ibn al-Ḥajj." He memorized and taught Ibn Mālik's famous didactic poem on grammar, comprising a thousand lines. He specifically taught his children this poem, emphasizing its importance among the religious subjects.

Imam al-Darʿī's student, al-Yūsī, remarked, "Once on Friday, I happened upon the imam in an area in the central mosque that scholars occupied. He had the seven famous pre-Islamic odes[3] with him and was correcting the text. I thought to myself, 'This is Friday, and the shaykh is sitting [with pre-Islamic poetry] in the teachers' area, which should be reserved for devotional practices on this day.' It was then that I realized he was of such profound spiritual excellence that for him, everything he did was devotional, because his intention was purely for the sake of God."[4]

---

2 *Kashf* is the term used in the original Arabic text and refers to a type of "revelation" that occurs for a saint, *walī*, which in no way should be likened to the revelation of prophets. It can be a recognition of someone's state that is hidden from others, or a "reading" of someone's thoughts, or it may take other forms. The person who has the unveiling may not necessarily be consciously aware of its occurrence, but one who is witnessing him will recognize it from him.

3 Serious study of classical Arabic requires thorough examination and understanding of these seven pre-Islamic odes (*al-Muʿallaqāt al-sabʿ*).

4 From an unpublished Moroccan mansuscript.

Imam al-Darʿī was also a master of horology and astronomy and was particularly adept at matters related to determining prayer times. Another example of the shaykh's penetrating insight and subtle ability to heal hearts occurred in connection with the astronomer and notable scholar Sīdī Muḥammad al-Mirghītī (d. 1090/1679), of Marrakech, who also wrote a highly praised commentary on the famous didactic poem of Abī Muqraʿ on astronomy, *al-Muqniʿ*. An established expert on prayer times, Imam al-Mirghītī was concerned that Imam al-Darʿī's disciples were praying the sunset prayer too early. Even though the shaykh's mosque had a minaret, the muezzin of the *zāwiyyah* used to give the call to prayer from a nearby hill. Once, when Imam al-Mirghītī was visiting Imam al-Darʿī, the host suggested they ascend the minaret to relax and take in the view. While up in the minaret, from where the setting sun could be seen, Imam al-Darʿī turned to his guest and said, "It would seem as if the time for sunset prayer has arrived." Just as Imam al-Mirghītī responded, "Yes," the muezzin on the hill began the call to prayer. After that, Imam al-Mirghītī used to say, "The muezzin at the *Nāṣirī Zāwiyyah* knows the prayer times like he knows his own sons."

Another testimony to Imam al-Darʿī's excellence comes from his student Imam al-Yūsī. Despite his own high stature and exalted knowledge, Imam al-Yūsī was in awe of his teacher. After Imam al-Yūsī made his pilgrimage to Mecca, he wrote that he could not find anyone of Imam al-Darʿī's stature in knowledge from whom he could benefit. This should suffice as a decisive proof of Imam al-Darʿī's vast knowledge, for Imam al-Yūsī was recognized as one of the greatest savants of his age, yet he considered himself far inferior to his teacher in both spiritual state and exoteric knowledge.

Imam al-Yūsī wrote extensively about his shaykh, including a biography in his *al-Fihrisah* and again in *The Lectures*. He also composed an encomium to the imam of 300 verses. In it, he wrote,

Creation's restoring rain, Nāṣir's son,
by him God granted victory to Aḥmad's way,

Restoring its essence to purity, clarity;
glorious, the delight of all Unitarians' eyes,

Raising its frame's roof until it rose
above celestial Spica's ascent over firm mountains.

Imam al-Darʿī is indeed a giant among the luminaries of Islam. His sincerity and his indefatigable efforts, coupled with his encyclopedic grasp of the sciences of Islam, rank him among the greatest scholars and spiritual sages of Morocco. He will, however, be most remembered for his extraordinary invocation, *The Prayer of the Oppressed*. It is his personal response to the terrible conditions under which Muslims of his age lived.

The invocation has served Moroccans well over the years: elderly Moroccans today even attribute to it the French withdrawal from Morocco in the mid-20th century. Shaykh Abdal Hayy al-Imrawi, the erudite grammarian of Fes, told me that this invocation was widely recited during the French occupation, and that the French authorities were so troubled by its power over the people, and by the people's belief in its efficacy, that they prohibited its recitation in the mosques; but Moroccans persisted nonetheless, to the chagrin of their occupiers. The Moroccan resistance to the French, both spiritual and martial, was unflagging, and, despite great loss of life and limb—far more on the Moroccan side than on the French—it led finally to the French withdrawal from the land of Imam Ibn Nāṣir al-Darʿī.

The power of the prayer lies in its simplicity, its purity, and its sincere supplication. It is essentially a plea to God that our transgressions (which invariably bring on the calamities we suffer) be overlooked, that divine mercy be bestowed upon us, that social justice be restored in spite of us, that wrongs be righted, and that righteousness reign once again in our lands, so that the destitute may no longer be in need and the young may be educated, the animals' purpose fulfilled, rain restored, and bounties poured forth. It is a plea to be freed from the aggression of foreigners in lands over which they have no right—a plea much needed in our modern world, rampant as it is with invasions and territorial occupations. Ultimately, it asks not that our enemies be destroyed but simply that their plots, and the harm they cause, be halted. Its essence is mercy, which in turn is the essence of the Messenger of God, Muḥammad ﷺ: "And We have only sent you as a mercy to all the worlds" (Qur'an, 21:107).

About This Translation and Recording

IMAM AL-DARʿĪ WROTE this prayer in a simple yet enchanting style, using the *rajaz* meter, which is known to the Arabs as the "poet's donkey" because of its facile rhythm and the ease even tyros find in learning it. The desert cameleers, who led the caravans of old, traditionally sang in the *rajaz* meter and by it spurred on their beasts to move more swiftly toward their destination. Arab poets claim the rhythm of the *rajaz* imitates the rhythm of the camel's trot and is, they believe, derived from it.

Rhetorically, the poem displays what the Arabs call "the easy impossible": deceptively simple thought and language which beguiles the listener into believing that such poetry is easy to write; yet upon any attempt at imitation, the aspirant is left thoroughly nonplussed. Poets know this magical aspect of "the craft" all too well. It would not be an exaggeration to say that there is no invocation in the Arabic language written in such simple yet subtle verse as Imam al-Darʿī's prayer.

When translating Imam al-Darʿī's invocation, I first put it into iambic pentameter, but I found great difficulty conveying the meanings precisely. So I decided to use hexameter, even though it is seldom used in English, because the doubling of the trimeter becomes repetitious and can easily devolve into doggerel. However, I chose it in order to convey something of the feel of the original *rajaz* meter, for which hexameter is the closest English equivalent. (The reader should note, however, that Arabic verse is quantitative: the rhythm is produced by the length of syllables, not by their accent, as in English.)

After considerable work on the translation, feeling quite satisfied with the result, I sent it to the American poet Daniel Abdal-Hayy Moore, who had helped so wonderfully in our previous collaboration on *The Poem of the Cloak (al-Burdah)*. Initially, he was troubled by the hexameter, and understandably so; but he decided to work with it and, in my opinion, helped me turn a donkey into a mule, for which I am deeply grateful. But the original is a thoroughbred, and for those who do not know Arabic, I highly recommend listening to the original as chanted so masterfully by the Fes Singers, led by Sīdī Mohammed Bennis.

Speaking of the recording, I feel compelled to relate an extraordinary incident, something I consider a miracle really. It is safe to say that this poem is noted for its miraculous nature, and Moroccans who are regular in their recitation of it will confirm that belief. On the night we finished the recording in Fes, it was quiet and still when we emerged from the studio into the cool night air and went for a late dinner. Then, at around three o'clock in the morning, Sīdī Abdallateef Whiteman (who also did the cover design and layout for this book) and I set out for our hotel in a car, with Mohammed Bennis and his fellow singers. We intended to pick up our bags and leave immediately for the taxi stand outside Bab Boujloud. A thoughtful friend from England had entrusted me with a monetary gift to deliver to Sīdī Ismail Filali, a sincere servant of God who lives in Fes, spending his days carding wool and his nights calling on God. Because we had to catch an early flight from Tangiers later that day and had a drive of several hours ahead of us, I knew I would not have time to visit Sīdī Ismail and deliver the gift; so I asked Sīdī Mohammed if he would do it. No sooner had I completed the question than we happened to pass by a large, windowless van with a man standing alongside it. It must have been 3:30 AM by now. Sīdī Mohammed exclaimed, "That looks just like Sīdī Ismail!"

We swung the car around and went back to find that, sure enough, it was Sīdī Ismail. We greeted each other, embracing warmly, and Sīdī Ismail exclaimed, "Glory to God! We just finished the *Burdah* and a recitation of the Qur'an in its entirety, and in the closing supplication, I asked God to see you tonight! By God, I swear it is true, and I did not know you were in Morocco." I had barely absorbed the import of what he told me when another surprise awaited me. Sīdī Ismail opened the back door of the van, revealing about ten spiritual seekers with radiant faces. As if conducting an orchestra, Sīdī Ismail raised his hands, and as he brought them down, the entire group broke into a spontaneous rendition of the prayer of Imam al-Darʿī, the very prayer we had just finished recording with the Fes Singers. This much is true: Sīdī Ismail had no knowledge that I was in Morocco at that time, nor that we had just completed the recording of the prayer of Imam al-Darʿī. God is my Witness.

Upon returning to the United States with the recording, I asked my blessed sister in faith, Aishah Holland, if she would pen the poem in its original Arabic for me. She had been a student of the American master of calligraphy, that most learned and accomplished polymath Mohamed Zakariya, who had recommended her highly. After she completed her work, my task was largely done, but there remained one missing piece: I had hoped to include the poem's chain of transmission back to Imam al-Darʿī, for the blessing of its lineage and the *barakah* of its narrators. I asked a close friend and scholar who had the chain, but a few years passed, and it was not forthcoming. I thought perhaps that I should not put the work out, that it was something not meant to be, as I felt insistent on acquiring the chain as permission from its author, so to speak.

On a blessed journey to Medina some years later, I was riding in a car in the middle of the Arabian desert with my teacher and dearest friend, Shaykh Abdallah bin Bayyah, a master of both the inward and outward sciences, and mentioned to him that I had translated the poem of Imam al-Darʿī. He smiled and said, "He is in my chain from my father." I then boldly requested from him the chain of transmission. He looked at me and said, "God willing." Time passed, and no chain came. I was beginning to believe that the poem would remain in my large collection of incomplete works. Then, on a more recent trip, as I was leaving for Medina again from Shaykh Abdallah bin Bayyah's house in Jeddah, he gave me the chain, and I felt it was time to release this poem.

May God accept it as a work of devotion that benefits believers and gives them solace in their trials and tribulations.

License to Transmit al-Du^cā' al-Nāṣirī

I HAVE RECEIVED this blessed supplication, *al-Du^cā' al-Nāṣirī*, aurally and with a written license with a chain of transmission that is linked to its author through my shaykh, the savant, the righteous spiritual master, distinct among his generation, singular in his era, my foundation, Shaykh Abdullah bin Bayyah, may God preserve him and make His providence to reign upon him. He narrated it to me on the authority of his father, the Shaykh, the polymath, the axial saint, al-Maḥfūẓ b. Bayyah; from Shaykh Muḥammad Maḥmūd b. Bayyah; from Shaykh ᶜĀlī b. Āfah; from Shaykh Muḥammad Maḥmūd, known also as al-Khalaf; from his father, Shaykh Sīdī Aḥmad b. ᶜUmar, known also as Shaykhunā al-Kabīr (our Eminent Shaykh); from Shaykh al-Mukhtār; from Shaykh Muḥammad al-Aqẓaf b. Ḥimā Allāh; from Zayn al-ᶜĀbidīn b. Sīdī Aḥmad; who narrated it from his father, the Shaykh, the Imam, the Gnostic, Sīdī Muḥammad b. Nāṣir al-Darᶜī, may God be pleased with all of them.

إسنادُ الدُعاءُ النَاصِري

تلقيت هذا الدعاء المبارك الدعاء النّاصري
قراءةً و إجازةً بالسّند المتّصل إلىٰ مؤلّفه عن شيخي
العلّامة الرّبّاني الفرد الصمداني فريد عصره و وحيد
دهره عمدتي الشّيخ عبد الله بن بيّه حفظه الله
وأدام تأييده عن والده الشّيخ العلّامة القطب الرّبّاني
المحفوظ بن بيّه عن الشّيخ محمّد محمود
ابن بيّه عن الشيخ عالي بن آفه عن الشيخ محمّد
محمود الملقّب الخالف عن والده الشّيخ سيدي
أحمد بن عمر الملقّب شيخنا الكبير عن الشّيخ
المختار عن الشّيخ محمّد الاقظف بن حمىٰ الله عن
زين العابدين بن سيدي أحمد عن أبيه
الشّيخ الإمام العارف سيدي محمّد بن ناصر
الدّرعي رضي الله عنهم جميعا

THE PRAYER *of* THE OPPRESSED

THE SWORD OF VICTORY'S LOT
OVER EVERY TYRANNY AND PLOT

Imam Muḥammad b. Nāṣir al-Darʿī

For oppression's victims everywhere,
Whose only weapon is earnest prayer.

Reckon not that God is heedless of the oppressors; rather He defers their punishment to a day in which eyes roll over and intellects evanesce.

—QUR'AN, 14:42

Guard yourselves against oppression and so protect your souls from the cry of the oppressed; for surely no barrier exists between the cry of the oppressed and God—even if that cry should come from an atheist.

—THE PROPHET MUḤAMMAD ﷺ

Supplication is the true weapon of a believer.

—THE PROPHET MUḤAMMAD ﷺ

الدُّعَاءُ النَّاصِرِيُّ

لِلْإِمَامِ الْعَارِفِ

سَيِّدِي مُحَمَّدُ بْنُ نَاصِرٍ الدَّرْعِي رَضِيَ اللهُ عَنْهُ

Prelude

I seek refuge in God from Satan, the accursed.

In the Name of God, the Beneficent, the Merciful.

Surely, God and His Angels bestow benedictions upon the Prophet. O all you of faith, bless him and salute him with sincere salutation. (33:56)

أَعُوذُ بِاللّٰهِ مِنَ الشَّيْطَانِ الرَّجِيمِ

بِسْمِ اللّٰهِ الرَّحْمٰنِ الرَّحِيمِ

إِنَّ اللّٰهَ وَمَلٰٓئِكَتَهُ يُصَلُّونَ عَلَى النَّبِيِّ يٰٓأَيُّهَا الَّذِينَ اٰمَنُوا

صَلُّوا عَلَيْهِ وَسَلِّمُوا تَسْلِيمًا

Dedication

To You, God of the Throne, I raise my only plea,
To confess to You, my Lord, what others cannot see.

My Lord, by Your Presence, treat and remedy
My heart and the disease, O efface this misery.

I can't enumerate the blessings You've bestowed—
Forbid, my God, my pardon from being withheld.

And if You don't save me from this living hell,
What will become of me? Can anyone foretell?

O God, You are the Real, my port, my only grace—
My heart's true love above this dark and deadly place.

إِلَيْكَ إِلَهَ العَرْشِ أَرْفَعُ حَاجَتِي

وَأُفْضِي بِمَا عَنْ كُلِّ خَلْقِكَ أَكْتُمُ

فَيَا رَبِّ زِدْنِي مِنْكَ صَبْراً وَدَاوِنِي

فَمِنْكَ دَوَاءُ مَا أَشْتَكِي وَبَلْسَمُ

وَكَمْ لَكَ مِنْ فَضْلٍ عَلَيَّ وَمِنَّةٍ

وَحَاشَاكَ أَرْجُو مِنْكَ عَفْواً فَأُحْرَمُ

إِذَا لَمْ تَكُنْ لِي فِي الصِّعَابِ فَمَنْ تُرَى

يَكُونُ لَعَمْرِي مِنْكَ مَا لَسْتُ أَفْهَمُ

فَأَنْتَ الإِلَهُ الحَقُّ مَا لِي مَوْئِلٌ

سِوَاكَ وَمَا لِلْقَلْبِ غَيْرُكَ يَرْحَمُ

The Prayer of the Oppressed

1. O You, whose mercy is a refuge for all those
In dire need who flee to You to lose their woes,

2. O master of reprieve, whose pardon is so near,
You answer all in need; they know that You do hear!

3. We beg for Your relief, redeemer of the weak;
You are enough for us, both humbled and so meek.

4. No strength can ever match Your awesome majesty,
No might can ever breach Your just authority.

5. The kings all bow like us to Your great sovereignty,
You choose whom to abase or raise decisively.

6. Calamities we face are only stopped by You;
It's in Your Hands: they are dissolved within Your view.

7. For solace in these states, we turn to You alone,
Complaining that we cannot make it on our own.

8. Be merciful with us—You know our frailty.
O You whose mercy falls like rain unceasingly,

9. Please look upon us now in all our misery,
Our state as souls oppressed displayed so openly:

يَا مَنْ إِلَى رَحْمَتِهِ ٱلْمَفَرُّ — وَمَنْ إِلَيْهِ يَلْجَأُ ٱلْمُضْطَرُّ

وَيَا قَرِيبَ ٱلْعَفْوِ يَا مَوْلَاهُ — وَيَا مُغِيثَ كُلِّ مَنْ دَعَاهُ

بِكَ ٱسْتَغَثْنَا يَا مُغِيثَ ٱلضُّعَفَا — فَحَسْبُنَا يَا رَبِّ أَنْتَ وَكَفَى

فَلَا أَجَلَّ مِنْ عَظِيمِ قُدْرَتِكْ — وَلَا أَعَزَّ مِنْ عَزِيزِ سَطْوَتِكْ

لِعِزِّ مُلْكِكَ ٱلْمُلُوكُ تَخْضَعُ — تَخْفِضُ قَدْرَ مَنْ تَشَا وَتَرْفَعُ

وَٱلْأَمْرُ كُلُّهُ إِلَيْكَ رَدُّهُ — وَبِيَدَيْكَ حَلُّهُ وَعَقْدُهُ

وَقَدْ رَفَعْنَا أَمْرَنَا إِلَيْكَ — وَقَدْ شَكَوْنَا ضَعْفَنَا عَلَيْكَ

فَارْحَمْنَا يَا مَنْ لَا يَزَالُ عَالِمَا — بِضَعْفِنَا وَلَا يَزَالُ رَاحِمَا

أُنْظُرْ إِلَى مَا مَسَّنَا مِنَ ٱلْوَرَى — فَحَالُنَا مِنْ بَيْنِهِمْ كَمَا تَرَى

10. Our numbers are reduced, our former wealth effaced,
Our once exalted rank and high repute abased;

11. They think us without strength, and deem us without power,
Our numbers in their eyes seem easy to devour.

12. O You whose mighty kingdom never becomes less,
We hope to take asylum in divine largesse;

13. Haven of the helpless, upon You we depend;
Helper of the hapless, we trust in Your godsend!

14. You are the one we call: relieve our heavy loads,
Repel our life's travails, abolish what corrodes!

15. Your protection only, Your providence that's true,
The door is Yours alone that everything comes through.

16. You are the only one whose bounteous door we seek,
Most generous of givers, O Lord, You are unique.

17. You bring us to the path should we all go astray
And overlook our slips when we lose our way;

18. All created things You hold in Your embrace,
With mercy and with light, the compass of Your grace.

19. Nothing in existence is able to compare
With just how base we are in mortality's affair.

قد قلّ جمعنا وقلّ وفرنا ... وانحطّ ما بين الجموع قدرنا

واستضعفونا شوكةً وشدّه ... واستنقصونا عُدّةً وعدّه

فنحن يا من ملكه لا يُسلب ... لذنا بجاهك الذي لا يُغلب

إليك يا غوث الفقير نستند ... عليك يا كهف الضعيف نعتمد

أنت الذي ندعو لكشف الغمرات ... أنت الذي نرجو لدفع الحسرات

أنت العناية التي لا نرتجي ... حماية من غير بابها تجي

أنت الذي نسعى بباب فضله ... أكرم من أغنى بفيض نيله

أنت الذي تهدي إذا ضللنا ... أنت الذي تعفو إذا زللنا

وسعت كلّ ما خلقت علماً ... ورأفةً ورحمةً وحلماً

وليس منّا في الوجود أحقر ... ولا لما عندك منّا أفقر

20. O infinite in beauty, whose endless good befalls
The creatures You have made, so answer all our calls!

21. You alone save drowning souls, so gracious with our states,
Rescuing the doomed, relieving our dire straits:

22. Constriction is increasing, there is no cure in sight,
So hasten to our needs, respond to set them right!

23. Our hands are raised to You, our palms are open wide:
We seek sincerely endless grace You do provide.

24. Be gentle with our souls in all You have decreed,
Bestow on us what pleases You in what we need.

25. Replace our state of hardship with Your gentle ease,
And guide us with Your power's prevailing breeze,

26. And place our status over those who took our lands,
Constrain their evil now, and tightly bind their hands;

27. Overcome our foes with Your subduing might,
Unravel all their hopes, and force them to take flight;

28. Deter their evil aims, and dash their unjust plan;
Repel them from our gates, and mystify each man.

29. Be swift in justice, Lord, in this our anxious hour,
For they cannot remove an atom of Your power.

يَا وَاسِعَ ٱلْإِحْسَانِ يَا مَنْ خَيْرُهُ   عَمَّ ٱلْوَرَى وَلَا يُنَادَى غَيْرُهُ

يَا مُنْقِذَ ٱلْغَرْقَى وَيَا حَنَّانُ   يَا مُنْجِيَ ٱلْهَلْكَى وَيَا مَنَّانُ

ضَاقَ ٱلنِّطَاقُ يَا سَمِيعُ يَا مُجِيبْ   عَزَّ ٱلدَّوَاءُ يَا سَرِيعُ يَا قَرِيبْ

وَقَدْ مَدَدْنَا رَبَّنَا ٱلْأَكُفَّ   وَمِنْكَ رَبَّنَا رَجَوْنَا ٱللُّطْفَ

فَالْطُفْ بِنَا فِيمَا بِهِ قَضَيْتَ   وَرَضِّنَا بِمَا بِهِ رَضِيتَ

وَأَبْدِلِ ٱللَّهُمَّ حَالَ ٱلْعُسْرِ   بِالْيُسْرِ وَامْدُدْنَا بِرِيحِ ٱلنَّصْرِ

وَاجْعَلْ لَنَا عَلَى ٱلْبُغَاةِ ٱلْغَلَبَهْ   وَاقْصُرْ أَذَى ٱلشَّرِّ عَلَى مَنْ طَلَبَهْ

وَاقْهَرْ عِدَانَا يَا عَزِيزُ قَهْرَا   يَفْصِمُ حَبْلَهُمْ وَيُصْمِي ٱلظَّهْرَا

وَاعْكِسْ مُرَادَهُمْ وَخَيِّبْ سَعْيَهُمْ   وَاهْزِمْ جُيُوشَهُمْ وَأَفْسِدْ رَأْيَهُمْ

وَعَجِّلِ ٱللَّهُمَّ فِيهِمْ نِقْمَتَكْ   فَإِنَّهُمْ لَا يُعْجِزُونَ قُدْرَتَكْ

30. O Lord, by holding on to Your most gracious rope,
We bind it to our faith, and knot it to our hope.

31. So stand for us today, don't counter what we try,
Forsake us not, O Lord, the blinking of an eye.

32. We're powerless to stop this onslaught of their force,
Or strategize to benefit our country's course.

33. We seek no good except what flows from Your wide door
And yearn for grace that comes from Your unending more.

34. All thoughts within our hearts will find serenity
Through God who fashions all by only saying: "*Be!*"

35. O Lord, by You alone, we will achieve our end,
By You, through You, Your means to You—our only friend.

36. Sustainer of us all, O towering support,
Our Lord who grants us all defense within His fort,

37. Secure our hearts within Your glorious defense,
In restless journeys far or in our residence;

38. Protect our herds, preserve our crops, increase our gains,
And give and bless our commerce with approving rains;

39. Fill our land with good prosperity,
Release our citizens from dire poverty;

يَا رَبِّ يَا رَبِّ بِحَبْلِ عِصْمَتِكَ	قَدِ اعْتَصَمْنَا وَبِعِزِّ نُصْرَتِكْ
فَكُنْ لَنَا وَلَا تَكُنْ عَلَيْنَا	وَلَا تَكِلْنَا طَرْفَةً إِلَيْنَا
فَمَا أَطَقْنَا قُوَّةً لِلدَّفْعِ	وَلَا اسْتَطَعْنَا حِيلَةً لِلنَّفْعِ
وَمَا قَصَدْنَا غَيْرَ بَابِكَ الْكَرِيمِ	وَمَا رَجَوْنَا غَيْرَ فَضْلِكَ الْعَمِيمِ
فَمَا رَجَتْ مِنْ خَيْرِكَ الظُّنُونُ	بِنَفْسِ مَا تَقُولُ كُنْ يَكُونُ
يَا رَبِّ يَا رَبِّ بِكَ التَّوَسُّلُ	لِمَا لَدَيْكَ وَبِكَ التَّوَسُّلُ
يَا رَبِّ أَنْتَ رُكْنُنَا الرَّفِيعُ	يَا رَبِّ أَنْتَ حِصْنُنَا الْمَنِيعُ
يَا رَبِّ يَا رَبِّ أَنِلْنَا الْأَمْنَا	إِذَا ارْتَحَلْنَا وَإِذَا أَقَمْنَا
يَا رَبِّ وَاحْفَظْ زَرْعَنَا وَضَرْعَنَا	وَاحْفَظْ تُجَّارَنَا وَفَرِّجْ جَمْعَنَا
وَاجْعَلْ بِلَادَنَا بِلَادَ الدِّينِ	وَرَاحَةَ الْمُحْتَاجِ وَالْمِسْكِينِ

40. Establish righteous rule while granting noble station,
With high respect and dignity in every nation;

41. Hide its natural strength in guarded secret trust,
And veil its protection in a graceful, gracious mist.

42. By the sacred sounds of *ṣad* and *qāf*, and holy *nūn*,
A thousand veils enfolding to protect our land from ruin,

43. By the rank of all the light from this Your Noble Face
And sacred estimation of Your vast dominion's space,

44. By the elevated rank of "*There is no god but God*"
And Your beloved chosen one who lived in purity, awed,

45. By the rank of every prophet, who ever called on You,
By the rank of every saint, who ever sought from You,

46. By the rank of humanity's blessèd Pole and Pillars too,
All solitary saints and inspired words[1] from You,

47. By the rank of those select and pious overseers,
Chosen spiritual substitutes for those departing here,

48. By the rank of faithful devotees who live in dignity,
Who praise their God in gratitude for His decree,

49. By the rank of everyone You raise to noble heights,
Among those You conceal or those You bring to light,

---

1 *Al-jaras* (or here, for the meter, *al-jars*) is the totality of divine expression that comes with unrelenting force. It is the divine reverberation of God's words penetrating the consciousness of the Prophet ﷺ. The Prophet ﷺ describes the most powerful form of revelation he experienced as the reverberation of a bell (*jaras*), and God knows best.

وَاجْعَلْ لَهَا بَيْنَ الْبِلَادِ صَوْلَهْ ... وَحُرْمَةً وَمَنْعَةً وَدَوْلَهْ

وَاجْعَلْ مِنَ السِّرِّ الْمَصُونِ عِزَّهَا ... وَاجْعَلْ مِنَ السِّتْرِ الْجَمِيلِ حِرْزَهَا

وَاجْعَلْ بِصَادٍ وَبِقَافٍ وَبِنُونْ ... أَلْفَ حِجَابٍ مِنْ وَرَائِهَا يَكُونْ

بِجَاهِ نُورِ وَجْهِكَ الْكَرِيمِ ... وَجَاهِ سِرِّ مُلْكِكَ الْعَظِيمِ

وَجَاهِ لَا إِلَهَ إِلَّا اللّٰهُ ... وَجَاهِ خَيْرِ الْخَلْقِ يَا رَبَّاهُ

وَجَاهِ مَا بِهِ دَعَاكَ الْأَنْبِيَا ... وَجَاهِ مَا بِهِ دَعَاكَ الْأَوْلِيَا

وَجَاهِ قَدْرِ الْقُطْبِ وَالْأَوْتَادِ ... وَجَاهِ حَالِ الْجَرْسِ وَالْأَفْرَادِ

وَجَاهِ الْأَخْيَارِ وَجَاهِ النُّجَبَا ... وَجَاهِ الْأَبْدَالِ وَجَاهِ النُّقَبَا

وَجَاهِ كُلِّ عَابِدٍ وَذَاكِرِ ... وَجَاهِ كُلِّ حَامِدٍ وَشَاكِرِ

وَجَاهِ كُلِّ مَنْ رَفَعْتَ قَدْرَهُ ... مِمَّنْ سَتَرْتَ أَوْ نَشَرْتَ ذِكْرَهُ

50. By the rank of every sign in Your Book's revelation
And the greatest name concealed in veiled occultation,

51. Lord, we stand before You now, bereft without You, lost,
Without design or strategy, by every tempest tossed;

52. We call on You with prayers of those who are infused
With knowledge that their Lord is One who won't refuse;

53. Accept this prayer, O Lord: with nothing but Your grace,
Remove all just deserts and show us mercy's face;

54. Reveal to us Your gifts, bestow on us Your favor
With kindness that befits a gentle, clement savior;

55. Envelop us, O Lord, within Your mercy's sea,
And rain on us Your grace that falls abundantly;

56. From all our words and deeds, choose those that remain
The highest and the best, so heaven is our gain;

57. O Plenitude, fill our lives and hearts with pure devotion,
In perfect harmony with Your Prophet's generous ocean,

58. And bring to focus all our aims into a single goal:
Complete and blissful knowledge of You within our soul!

59. Let us always act, Lord, in accord with Aḥmad's way,
Directing all our hopes to a joyful Judgment Day;

وَجَاهِ آيَاتِ الْكِتَابِ الْمُحْكَمِ   وَجَاهِ الِاسْمِ الْأَعْظَمِ الْمُعَظَّمِ

يَارَبِّ يَارَبِّ وَقَفْنَا فُقَرَا   بَيْنَ يَدَيْكَ ضُعَفَاءَ حُقَرَا

وَقَدْ دَعَوْنَاكَ دُعَاءَ مَنْ دَعَا   رَبًّا كَرِيمًا لَا يَرُدُّ مَنْ سَعَى

فَاقْبَلْ دُعَاءَنَا بِمَحْضِ الْفَضْلِ   قَبُولَ مَنْ أَلْغَى حِسَابَ الْعَدْلِ

وَامْنُنْ عَلَيْنَا مِنَّةَ الْكَرِيمِ   وَاعْطِفْ عَلَيْنَا عَطْفَةَ الْحَلِيمِ

وَانْشُرْ عَلَيْنَا يَا رَحِيمُ رَحْمَتَكْ   وَابْسُطْ عَلَيْنَا يَا كَرِيمُ نِعْمَتَكْ

وَخِرْ لَنَا فِي سَائِرِ الْأَقْوَالِ   وَاخْتَرْ لَنَا فِي سَائِرِ الْأَفْعَالِ

يَارَبِّ وَاجْعَلْ دَأْبَنَا التَّمَسُّكَا   بِالسُّنَّةِ الْغَرَّاءِ وَالتَّنَسُّكَا

وَاحْصُرْ لَنَا أَغْرَاضَنَا الْمُخْتَلِفَهْ   فِيكَ وَعَرِّفْنَا تَمَامَ الْمَعْرِفَهْ

وَاجْمَعْ لَنَا مَا بَيْنَ عِلْمٍ وَعَمَلْ   وَاصْرِفْ إِلَى دَارِ الْبَقَا مِنَّا الْأَمَلْ

60. Always lead us, Lord, to what is right and true,
The path real martyrs take and those who gaze on You;

61. Raise our children up as brave and pious scholars
Who base their days on Your sweet light as true exemplars;

62. And unify the hearts of family and of friends,
Facilitate for us in making our amends;

63. O Lord, bestow a clear decisive victory
On all who aid this way and restore its dignity;

64. Possessor of great might, aid him and those who serve,
And fill their hearts with aspirations they deserve;

65. Aid us in the light of this Muḥammad's way,
And make its glorious end as bright as its first day;

66. Protect it through the works of its faithful and true scholars
And elevate its lights to its rightful radiant colors;

67. Pardon and forgive us, and keep us safe from ill,
And all submitted ones who seek to know Your will;

68. Bestow Your lordly solace on the perfect Chosen One,
Your plenitudinous grace upon his dazzling sun;

69. Bestow on him a peace that befits his holy stature
In accordance with the pure nobility of his nature,

وَانْهَجْ بِنَا يَا رَبِّ نَهْجَ السُّعَدَا   وَاخْتِمْ لَنَا يَا رَبِّ خَتْمَ الشُّهَدَا

وَاجْعَلْ بَنِينَا فُضَلَاءَ صُلَحَا   وَعُلَمَاءَ عَامِلِينَ نُصَحَا

وَأَصْلِحِ اللَّهُمَّ حَالَ الْأَهْلِ   وَيَسِّرِ اللَّهُمَّ جَمْعَ الشَّمْلِ

يَا رَبِّ وَافْتَحْ فَتْحَكَ الْمُبِينَ   لِمَنْ تَوَلَّى وَأَعَزَّ الدِّينَ

وَانْصُرْهُ يَا ذَا الطَّوْلِ وَانْصُرْ حِزْبَهُ   وَامْلَأْ بِمَا يُرْضِيكَ عَنْهُ قَلْبَهُ

يَا رَبِّ وَانْصُرْ دِينَنَا الْمُحَمَّدِي   وَاجْعَلْ خِتَامَ عِزِّهِ كَمَا بُدِي

وَاحْفَظْهُ يَا رَبِّ بِحِفْظِ الْعُلَمَا   وَارْفَعْ مَنَارَ نُورِهِ إِلَى السَّمَا

وَاعْفُ وَعَافِ وَاكْفِ وَاغْفِرْ ذَنْبَنَا   وَذَنْبَ كُلِّ مُسْلِمٍ يَا رَبَّنَا

وَصَلِّ يَا رَبِّ عَلَى الْمُخْتَارِ   صَلَاتَكَ الْكَامِلَةَ الْمِقْدَارِ

صَلَاتَكَ الَّتِي تَفِي بِأَمْرِهِ   كَمَا يَلِيقُ بِارْتِفَاعِ قَدْرِهِ

70. And on his noble family down the ages, everyone,
Companions, followers, every daughter, every son.

71. Praise belongs to God alone, with a praise so direct
All praising seekers find their goal among the elect.

ثُمَّ عَلَى الْآلِ الكِرَامِ وَعَلَى   أَصْحَابِهِ الغُرِّ وَمَنْ لَهُمْ تَلَا

وَالحَمْدُ لِلَّهِ الَّذِي بِحَمْدِهِ   يَبْلُغُ ذُو القَصْدِ تَمَامَ قَصْدِهِ

The Prayer of the Oppressed

WITH TRANSLITERATED TEXT

Prelude

Aʿūdhu bi l-lāhi mina sh-shayṭāni r-rajīm
I seek refuge in God from Satan, the accursed.

bismi l-lāhi r-raḥmāni r-raḥīm
In the Name of God, the Beneficent, the Merciful.

inna l-lāha wa malā'ikatahu yuṣallūna ʿalā n-nabī
Surely, God and His angels bestow benedictions
upon the Prophet.

yā ayyuhā l-ladhīna āmanū ṣallū ʿalayhi wa sallimū taslīmā
O all you of faith, bless him and salute him
with sincere salutation. (33:56)

Ṣalla l-lāhu ʿalayka wa ʿalā ālika wa sallam. Allāhumma ṣalli ṣalātan kāmilatan wa sallim salāman tāmman ʿalā sayyidinā Muḥammad, al-ladhī tanḥallu bihi l-ʿuqad, wa tanfariju bihi l-kurab, wa tuqḍā bihi l-ḥawā'ij, wa tunālu bihi r-raghā'ib, wa ḥusnu l-khawātim, wa yustasqā l-ghamāmu bi wajhihi l-karīm, wa ʿalā ālihi wa ṣaḥbih, fī kulli lamḥatin wa nafasin bi ʿadadi kulli maʿlūmin laka yā Allāh.

May God bestow upon you and your family benedictions and salutations. O God, shower our master, Muḥammad, with the full extent of mercy, and with the full expanse of serenity, by whom all entanglements are disentangled, by whom all distress is allayed, by whom all needs are met, by whom all aspirations are achieved, by whom our final deeds are adorned, and by whose noble face are clouds petitioned to give drink; and upon his family and companions, with the blink of every eye and with every breath, as reaches the number of every thing known to You, O God!

Dedication

Ilayka ilāha l-ʿarshi arfaʿu ḥājatī
wa ufḍī bimā ʿan kulli khalqika aktumu

To You, God of the Throne, I raise my only plea,
To confess to You, my Lord, what others cannot see.

fa yā rabbi zidnī minka ṣabran wa dāwinī
fa minka dawā mā ashtakīhi wa balsamu

My Lord, by Your Presence, treat and remedy
My heart and the disease, O efface this misery.

wa kam laka min faḍlin ʿalayya wa minnatin
wa ḥāshāka arjū minka ʿafwan fa uḥramu

I can't enumerate the blessings You've bestowed—
Forbid, my God, my pardon from being withheld.

idhā lam takun lī fī ṣ-ṣiʿābi faman turā
yakūnu laʿamrī laka mā lastu afhamu

And if You don't save me from this living hell,
What will become of me? Can anyone foretell?

fa anta l-ilāhu l-ḥaqqu mā liya maw'ilun
siwāka wa mā li l-qalbi ghayruka yarḥamu

O God, You are the Real, my port, my only grace—
My heart's true love above this dark and deadly place.

The Prayer of the Oppressed

1. *Yā man ilā raḥmatihi l-mafarru*
wa man ilayhi yalja'u l-muḍṭarru

O You, whose mercy is a refuge for all those
In dire need who flee to You to lose their woes,

2. *wa yā qarība l-ʿafwi yā mawlāhu*
wa yā mughītha kulli man daʿāhu

O master of reprieve, whose pardon is so near,
You answer all in need; they know that You do hear!

3. *bika-staghathnā yā mughītha ḍ-ḍuʿafā*
fa ḥasbunā yā rabbi anta wa kafā

We beg for Your relief, redeemer of the weak;
You are enough for us, both humbled and so meek.

4. *fa lā ajalla min ʿaẓīmi qudratik*
wa lā aʿazza min ʿazīzi saṭwatik

No strength can ever match Your awesome majesty,
No might can ever breach Your just authority.

5. *li ʿizzi mulkika l-mulūku takhḍaʿu*
takhfiḍu qadra man tashā wa tarfaʿu

The kings all bow like us to Your great sovereignty,
You choose whom to abase or raise decisively.

6. *wa l-amru kulluhu ilayka radduhu*
wa bi yadayka ḥalluhu wa ʿaqduhu

Calamities we face are only stopped by You;
It's in Your Hands: they are dissolved within Your view.

7. *wa qad rafaʿnā amranā ilayka*
wa qad shakawnā ḍuʿfanā ʿalayka

For solace in these states, we turn to You alone,
Complaining that we cannot make it on our own.

8. *fa-rḥamnā yā man lā yazālu ʿālimā*
bi ḍuʿfinā wa lā yazālu rāḥimā

Be merciful with us—You know our frailty.
O You whose mercy falls like rain unceasingly,

9. *unẓur ilā mā massanā mina l-warā*
fa ḥāluna min baynihim kamā tarā

Please look upon us now in all our misery,
Our state as souls oppressed displayed so openly:

10. *qad qalla jamʿunā wa qalla wafrunā*
wa-nḥaṭṭa mā bayna l-jumūʿi qadrunā

Our numbers are reduced, our former wealth effaced,
Our once exalted rank and high repute abased;

11. *wa-staḍ^cafūnā shawkatan wa shiddah*
wa-stanqaṣūnā ʿuddatan wa ʿiddah

They think us without strength, and deem us without power,
Our numbers in their eyes seem easy to devour.

12. *fa naḥnu yā man mulkuhu lā yuslabu*
ludhnā bi jāhika l-ladhī lā yughlabu

O You whose mighty kingdom never becomes less,
We hope to take asylum in divine largesse;

13. *ilayka yā ghawtha l-faqīri nastanid*
ʿalayka yā kahfa ḍ-ḍaʿīfi naʿtamid

Haven of the helpless, upon You we depend;
Helper of the hapless, we trust in Your godsend!

14. *anta l-ladhī nadʿū li kashfi l-ghamarāt*
anta l-ladhī narjū li dafʿi l-ḥasarāt

You are the one we call: relieve our heavy loads,
Repel our life's travails, abolish what corrodes!

15. *anta l-ʿināyatu l-latī lā nartajī*
ḥimāyatan min ghayri bābihā tajī

Your protection only, Your providence that's true,
The door is Yours alone that everything comes through.

16. *anta l-ladhī nasʿā bi bābi faḍlihi*
akramu man aghnā bi fayḍi naylihi

You are the only one whose bounteous door we seek,
Most generous of givers, O Lord, You are unique.

17. *anta l-ladhī tahdī idhā ḍalalnā*
anta l-ladhī taʿfū idhā zalalnā

You bring us to the path should we all go astray
And overlook our slips when we lose our way;

18. *wasiʿta kulla mā khalaqta ʿilmā*
wa ra'fatan wa raḥmatan wa ḥilmā

All created things You hold in Your embrace,
With mercy and with light, the compass of Your grace.

19. *wa laysa minnā fī l-wujūdi aḥqaru*
wa lā limā ʿindaka minnā afqaru

Nothing in existence is able to compare
With just how base we are in mortality's affair.

20. *yā wāsiʿa l-iḥsāni yā man khayruhu*
ʿamma l-warā wa lā yunādā ghayruhu

O infinite in beauty, whose endless good befalls
The creatures You have made, so answer all our calls!

21. *yā munqidha l-gharqā wa yā ḥannānu*
yā munjiya l-halkā wa yā mannānu

You alone save drowning souls, so gracious with our states,
Rescuing the doomed, relieving our dire straits:

22. *ḍāqa n-niṭāqu yā samīʿu yā mujīb*
ʿazza d-dawā'u yā sarīʿu yā qarīb

Constriction is increasing, there is no cure in sight,
So hasten to our needs, respond to set them right!

23. *wa qad madadnā rabbanā l-akuffa*
wa minka rabbanā rajawnā l-luṭfa

Our hands are raised to You, our palms are open wide:
We seek sincerely endless grace You do provide.

24. *fa-lṭuf binā fīmā bihi qaḍayta*
wa raḍḍinā bimā bihi raḍīta

Be gentle with our souls in all You have decreed,
Bestow on us what pleases You in what we need.

25. *wa abdili l-lāhumma ḥāla l-ʿusri*
bi l-yusri wa-mdudnā bi rīḥi n-naṣri

Replace our state of hardship with Your gentle ease,
And guide us with Your power's prevailing breeze,

26. *wa-jʿal lanā ʿalā l-bughāti l-ghalabah*
wa-qṣur adhā sh-sharri ʿalā man ṭalabah

And place our status over those who took our lands,
Constrain their evil now, and tightly bind their hands;

27. *wa-qhar ʿidānā yā ʿazīzu qahrā*
yafṣimu ḥablahum wa yuṣmī ẓ-ẓahrā

Overcome our foes with Your subduing might,
Unravel all their hopes, and force them to take flight;

28. *wa-ʿkis murādahum wa khayyib saʿyahum*
wa-hzim juyūshahum wa afsid ra'yahum

Deter their evil aims, and dash their unjust plan;
Repel them from our gates, and mystify each man.

29. *wa ʿajjili l-lāhumma fīhim niqmatak*
fa innahum lā yuʿjizūna qudratak

Be swift in justice, Lord, in this our anxious hour,
For they cannot remove an atom of Your power.

30. *yā rabbi yā rabbi bi ḥabli ʿiṣmatik*
qadi-ʿtaṣamnā wa bi ʿizzi nuṣratik

O Lord, by holding on to Your most gracious rope,
We bind it to our faith, and knot it to our hope.

31. *fa kun lanā wa lā takun ʿalaynā*
wa lā takilnā ṭarfatan ilaynā

So stand for us today, don't counter what we try,
Forsake us not, O Lord, the blinking of an eye.

32. *fa mā aṭaqnā quwwatan li d-dafʿi*
wa lā-staṭaʿnā ḥīlatan li n-nafʿi

We're powerless to stop this onslaught of their force,
Or strategize to benefit our country's course.

33. *wa mā qaṣadnā ghayra bābika l-karīm*
wa mā rajawnā ghayra faḍlika l-ʿamīm

We seek no good except what flows from Your wide door
And yearn for grace that comes from Your unending more.

34. *fa mā rajat min khayrika ẓ-ẓunūnu*
bi nafsi mā taqūlu kun yakūnu

All thoughts within our hearts will find serenity
Through God who fashions all by only saying: "*Be!*"

35. *yā rabbi yā rabbi bika t-tawaṣṣulu*
limā ladayka wa bika t-tawassulu

O Lord, by You alone, we will achieve our end,
By You, through You, Your means to You—our only friend.

36. *yā rabbi anta ruknunā r-rafīʿu*
yā rabbi anta ḥiṣnunā l-manīʿu

Sustainer of us all, O towering support,
Our Lord who grants us all defense within His fort,

37. *yā rabbi yā rabbi anilnā l-amnā*
idhā-rtaḥalnā wa idhā aqamnā

Secure our hearts within Your glorious defense,
In restless journeys far or in our residence;

38. *yā rabbi wa-ḥfaẓ zarʿanā wa ḍarʿanā*
wa-ḥfaẓ tijāranā wa waffir jamʿanā

Protect our herds, preserve our crops, increase our gains,
And give and bless our commerce with approving rains;

39. *wa-jʿal bilādanā bilāda d-dīni*
wa rāḥata l-muḥtāji wa l-miskīni

Fill our land with good prosperity,
Release our citizens from dire poverty;

40. *wa-jʿal lahā bayna l-bilādi ṣawlah*
wa ḥurmatan wa manʿatan wa dawlah

Establish righteous rule while granting noble station,
With high respect and dignity in every nation;

41. *wa-jᶜal mina s-sirri l-maṣūni ᶜizzahā*
wa-jᶜal mina s-sitri l-jamīli ḥirzahā

Hide its natural strength in guarded secret trust,
And veil its protection in a graceful, gracious mist.

42. *wa-jᶜal bi ṣādin wa bi qāfin wa bi nūn*
alfa ḥijābin min warā'ihā yakūn

By the sacred sounds of *ṣad* and *qāf*, and holy *nūn*,
A thousand veils enfolding to protect our land from ruin,

43. *bi jāhi nūri wajhika l-karīmi*
wa jāhi sirri mulkika l-ᶜaẓīmi

By the rank of all the light from this Your Noble Face
And sacred estimation of Your vast dominion's space,

44. *wa jāhi lā ilāha illā l-lāhu*
wa jāhi khayri l-khalqi yā rabbāhu

By the elevated rank of "*There is no god but God*"
And Your beloved chosen one who lived in purity, awed,

45. *wa jāhi mā bihi daᶜāka l-anbiyā*
wa jāhi mā bihi daᶜāka l-awliyā

By the rank of every prophet, who ever called on You,
By the rank of every saint, who ever sought from You,

46. *wa jāhi qadri l-quṭbi wa l-awtādi*
wa jāhi ḥāli l-jarsi wa l-afrādi

By the rank of humanity's blessèd Pole and Pillars too,
All solitary saints and inspired words from You,

47. *wa jāhi l-akhyāri wa jāhi n-nujabā*
wa jāhi l-abdāli wa jāhi n-nuqabā

By the rank of those select and pious overseers,
Chosen spiritual substitutes for those departing here,

48. *wa jāhi kulli ʿābidin wa dhākir*
wa jāhi kulli ḥāmidin wa shākir

By the rank of faithful devotees who live in dignity,
Who praise their God in gratitude for His decree,

49. *wa jāhi kulli man rafaʿta qadrahu*
mim-man satarta aw nasharta dhikrahu

By the rank of everyone You raise to noble heights,
Among those You conceal or those You bring to light,

50. *wa jāhi āyāti l-kitābi l-muḥkami*
wa jāhi li-smi l-aʿẓami l-muʿaẓẓami

By the rank of every sign in Your Book's revelation
And the greatest name concealed in veiled occultation,

51. *yā rabbi yā rabbi waqafnā fuqarā*
bayna yadayka ḍuᶜafā'a ḥuqarā

Lord, we stand before You now, bereft without You, lost,
Without design or strategy, by every tempest tossed;

52. *wa qad daᶜawnāka duᶜā'a man daᶜā*
rabban karīman lā yaruddu man saᶜā

We call on You with prayers of those who are infused
With knowledge that their Lord is One who won't refuse;

53. *fa-qbal duᶜā'anā bi maḥḍi l-faḍli*
qabūla man alghā ḥisāba l-ᶜadli

Accept this prayer, O Lord: with nothing but Your grace,
Remove all just deserts and show us mercy's face;

54. *wa-mnun ᶜalaynā minnata l-karīmi*
wa-ᶜṭifᶜalaynā ᶜaṭfata l-ḥalīmi

Reveal to us Your gifts, bestow on us Your favor
With kindness that befits a gentle, clement savior;

55. *wa-nshur ᶜalaynā yā raḥīmu raḥmatak*
wa-bsuṭ ᶜalaynā yā karīmu niᶜmatak

Envelop us, O Lord, within Your mercy's sea,
And rain on us Your grace that falls abundantly;

56. *wa khir lanā fī sā'iri l-aqwāli*
wakhtar lanā fī sā'iri l-afʿāli

From all our words and deeds, choose those that remain
The highest and the best, so heaven is our gain;

57. *yā rabbi wa-jʿal da'banā t-tamassukā*
bi s-sunnati l-gharrā'i wa t-tanassukā

O Plenitude, fill our lives and hearts with pure devotion,
In perfect harmony with Your Prophet's generous ocean,

58. *wa-ḥṣur lanā aghrāḍanā l-mukhtalifah*
fīka wa ʿarrifnā tamāma l-maʿrifah

And bring to focus all our aims into a single goal:
Complete and blissful knowledge of You within our soul!

59. *wa-jmaʿ lanā mā bayna ʿilmin wa ʿamal*
wa-ṣrif ilā dāri l-baqā minnā l-amal

Let us always act, Lord, in accord with Aḥmad's way,
Directing all our hopes to a joyful Judgment Day;

60. *wa-nhaj binā yā rabbi nahja s-suʿadā*
wa-khtim lanā yā rabbi khatma sh-shuhadā

Always lead us, Lord, to what is right and true,
The path real martyrs take and those who gaze on You;

61. *wa-jʿal banīnā fuḍalā'a ṣulaḥā*
wa ʿulamā'a ʿāmilīna nuṣaḥā

Raise our children up as brave and pious scholars
Who base their days on Your sweet light as true exemplars;

62. *wa aṣliḥi l-lāhumma ḥāla l-ahli*
wa yassiri l-lāhumma jamʿa sh-shamli

And unify the hearts of family and of friends,
Facilitate for us in making our amends;

63. *yā rabbi wa-ftaḥ fatḥaka l-mubīna*
li man tawallā wa aʿazza d-dīna

O Lord, bestow a clear decisive victory
On all who aid this way and restore its dignity;

64. *wa-nṣurhu yā dhā ṭ-ṭawli wa-nṣur ḥizbahu*
wa-mla' bimā yurḍīka ʿanhu qalbahu

Possessor of great might, aid him and those who serve,
And fill their hearts with aspirations they deserve;

65. *yā rabbi wa-nṣur dīnanā l-Muḥammadī*
wa-jʿal khitāma ʿizzihi kamā budī

Aid us in the light of this Muḥammad's way,
And make its glorious end as bright as its first day;

66. *wa-ḥfaẓhu yā rabbi bi ḥifẓi l-ʿulamā*
wa-rfaʿ manāra nūrihi ilā s-samā

Protect it through the works of its faithful and true scholars
And elevate its lights to its rightful radiant colors;

67. *wa-ʿfu wa ʿāfi wa-kfi wa-ghfir dhambanā*
wa dhamba kulli muslimin yā rabbanā

Pardon and forgive us, and keep us safe from ill,
And all submitted ones who seek to know Your will;

68. *wa ṣalli yā rabbi ʿalā l-mukhtāri*
ṣalātaka l-kāmilata l-miqdāri

Bestow Your lordly solace on the perfect Chosen One,
Your plenitudinous grace upon his dazzling sun;

69. *ṣalātaka l-latī tafī bi amrihi*
kamā yalīqu bi-rtifāʿi qadrihi

Bestow on him a peace that befits his holy stature
In accordance with the pure nobility of his nature,

70. *thumma ʿalā l-āli l-kirāmi wa ʿalā*
aṣḥābihi l-ghurri wa man lahum talā

And on his noble family down the ages, everyone,
Companions, followers, every daughter, every son.

71. *wa l-ḥamdu li l-lāhi l-ladhī bi ḥamdihi*
yablughu dhū l-qaṣdi tamāma qaṣdihi

Praise belongs to God alone, with a praise so direct
All praising seekers find their goal among the elect.

Appendix on Intercession

TAWASSUL IS AN ARABIC word that comes from a verbal noun, *wasīlah*, which according to Ibn Manẓūr (d. 711/1311) in *Lisān al-ʿArab* means "a station with the king, a rank, or an act of devotion." In other words, it refers to a position of power due to one's proximity to the king or sovereign. In the Islamic tradition, it refers to an act that draws one near to God. A good example of *tawassul* is found in the well-known hadith of the young men trapped in a cave whose mouth was covered by a stone: Each man prays to God, and mentions some act that he did for God's sake, in hopes that it might cause his prayers to be accepted. This is *tawassul* with one's good actions, an agreed-upon practice among Muslims.

In fact, *tawassala ilayh* means, "to draw near through an action." Imam al-Rāghib al-Iṣfahānī says in his *al-Mufradāt* that its true meaning is drawing near to God in one's knowledge, in devotion, and in observing the noble virtues found in the sacred law. In other contexts, *tawassul* can actually mean "to steal something," as in, "He obtained the camels through theft" (*tawassulan*).

The word *al-wasīlah* is used in the Qur'anic verse: "Believers, be conscious of God, and seek to draw near (*al-wasīlah*) to God, and struggle for the sake of God that you might thrive" (5:35). Almost all the classical commentators, including the great Sufi exegetes, such as al-Qushayrī (d. 465/1074), explain the use of *al-wasīlah* in this verse to mean avoiding what is prohibited, fulfilling what is enjoined on us, and drawing near to God through good actions. Shaykh Ibn Taymiyyah (d.728/1328), in his work on the subject, *al-Tawassul wa al-wasīlah*, says:

> *Tawassul* has three meanings: The first is to draw near with one's acts of obedience, and this is an obligation without which faith is incomplete. The second is drawing near to God with the Prophet's prayers and his

> intercession, and this is only during his life and on the Day of Judgment, in which humanity seeks his *wasīlah* through his intercession. Finally, the third is to beseech God through the essence of the Prophet ﷺ and to supplicate through his essence. This last type was neither performed by the companions of the Prophet ﷺ in their rain prayers nor in any other type of prayer, neither during his life nor after his death, nor at his grave or anyone else's grave. Furthermore, it is not known in any of the famous prayers that the companions recited. It is simply found transmitted though weak hadith that are either traced back to the Prophet ﷺ or end with one of the companions or from someone whose words are not authoritative.[1]

This position is also related by some of the companions of Imam Mālik. Sīdī Aḥmad Zarrūq (d. 899/1493) says in *al-Qawāʿid*, "It is related that Mālik said, 'One should not use as a *wasīlah* a created thing (*bi makhlūq*).' And some add, except for the Messenger of God ﷺ."[2] This position is also cited as the position of Imam Abū Ḥanīfah (d. 150/767).

There are two problems with this position, however. The first is that all scholars agree that actions may be used as a *wasīlah* in our supplications, and the consensus of the scholars is that actions are created things. Hence the argument that the *createdness* of something is what causes its prohibition as a *wasīlah* is unsound. The other problem with this position is that there is no evidence indicating that the Prophet's intercession is only during his lifetime for his companions and on the Day of Judgment. This is clearly an opinion that Ibn Taymiyyah derived from the tradition which relates that Sayyidunā ʿUmar b. al-Khaṭṭāb ﷺ stated during a rain prayer, "O God, we used to use the Prophet ﷺ as a *wasīlah*, and now we are asking through his uncle, al-ʿAbbās." Ibn Taymiyyah's position assumes that Sayyidunā ʿUmar ﷺ did not intercede through the Prophet ﷺ because he considered it impermissible, but there is no evidence for that. In fact, this statement of Sayyidunā

1 Ibn Taymiyyah, *al-Tawassul wa al-wasīlah* (Beirut: Dār al-Fikr al-Lubnānī, 1992), 51.
2 Sīdī Aḥmad Zarrūq, *al-Qawāʿid* (Tunis: n.p., 1987), 80.

ʿUmar ؓ actually strengthens the position of the validity of intercession through the Prophet ﷺ, as the only reason he asked through Sayyidunā al-ʿAbbās ؓ is due to his close relationship to the Prophet ﷺ. Sayyidunā al-ʿAbbās ؓ was certainly not the best man in the gathering, as Sayyidunā ʿAlī ؓ and others whose rank is considered higher than Sayyidunā al-ʿAbbās were present.

Moreover, the absolutely sound hadith of Sayyidunā ʿUthmān b. Ḥunayf ؓ, which Shaykh Ibn Taymiyyah interpreted in an idiosyncratic way, is a clear example of a companion seeking the Prophet's intercession both during his lifetime and after his death. In addition, the Qur'an itself proves that the Prophet ﷺ is encouraged to ask forgiveness for his followers according to the verse, "And if they had only come to you seeking forgiveness of God when they had wronged themselves, and the Messenger had asked forgiveness for them, they would have found God most relenting, most merciful" (4:64).

According to a sound hadith narrated by al-Bazzār, the Prophet ﷺ stated, "My life is good for you, and my death is good for you. You do things, and things are revealed in response. But your actions will be shown to me in my grave. If I find good, I thank God, and if I find otherwise, I ask forgiveness for you." There is a disagreement about whether our actions are shown to the Prophet ﷺ individually or collectively, as a community, but what is important from this sound hadith is that the Prophet ﷺ asks forgiveness for us in his grave: hence, he intercedes for us after his death and before the Day of Judgment.

Furthermore, many scholars, including Imam al-Nawawī in his *al-Majmūʿ*, Qadi ʿIyāḍ (d. 544/1140) in his *al-Shifā'*, and Ibn Kathīr (d. 774/1373) in his Qur'anic exegesis, relate a story from Imam al-ʿUtbī (d. 255/869), who was one of the great scholars of the generation following that of the followers of the companions of the Prophet ﷺ (*tābiʿ al-tābiʿīn*). Imam al-ʿUtbī related that he heard a Bedouin say at the grave of the Prophet ﷺ, "Peace be upon you, O Messenger of God; I heard God say, 'And if they had only come to you…' [4:64], so here I am! I have come to you asking forgiveness of my sins from

God and seeking your intercession...." The Bedouin then recited some poetry and left. Thereafter, Imam al-ʿUtbī had a dream in which the Prophet ﷺ told him to find the Bedouin and inform him that God had forgiven him his sins. Lines of poetry commemorating this story remain on the two pillars of the Prophet's tomb. While this story is violently attacked in an editor's footnote as fabricated and idolatrous (*shirk*) in certain editions of Ibn Kathīr's Qur'anic exegesis, it seems extremely odd that the luminaries of Islam who all relate this story failed to notice the *shirk* involved in the story. Ibn Kathīr relates it with no comment, indicating that he approved of the narration, and he was Ibn Taymiyyah's student.

There are many more proofs for such practices, but suffice it to say that both positions are found in our tradition, and neither can claim absolute authority over the other. However, the dominant position of our community for centuries has been that asking the Prophet ﷺ to intercede on our behalf is neither prohibited nor *shirk*. Moreover, asking through a person with the rank of a scholar or saint is also permissible. Whether we are actually asking because of our good opinion of that person (which in essence is a good deed, as the Qur'an commands us to have a good opinion of others) is a moot point. What remains true is that *tawassul* is neither *shirk* nor prohibited, and Muslims who choose not to engage in *tawassul* should refrain from attacking other Muslims who choose to do so. Our tradition is vast and far more nuanced than many modern Muslims realize. Moreover, anyone who truly understands the Māturīdī and Ashʿarī positions on primary causation is absolutely incapable of *shirk*, and to accuse the greatest scholars of Islam, such as Imam al-Nawawī, of *shirk* in permitting *tawassul* is to jeopardize one's own faith.

Finally, Imam al-Darʿī, in his *Prayer of the Oppressed*, supplicates to God through the rank of the saints, who are referred to as the *Dīwān al-Awliyā'* (*Divan of Saints*), as a means of interceding with his Lord. This is not *shirk*, nor is it prohibited, but a minority opinion does oppose it. While we respect the minority's right to dissent from the majority opinion, we do not accept their anathematizing of Muslims who do invoke such a prayer.

Moreover, while the *Divan of Saints* is only alluded to in the Qur'an and in hadith literature, its existence has been affirmed by countless scholars, including Imam al-Suyūṭī, in his "*al-Khabar al-dāl ʿalā wujūd al-quṭb wa al-awtād wa al-nujabā wa al-abdāl.*" In this small treatise, he relates several sound hadith establishing the *Divan of Saints*. These saints comprise a fixed number of people at all times; hence, should one of them die, that person is replaced by one of the living righteous people. Three hundred of them are called *nujabā*, forty are called *nuqabā*, thirty are called *budalā* or *abdāl*, four are called *awtād*, and one is known as the *quṭb*, who is the most righteous man on earth at any given time. If the *quṭb* dies, he is replaced by one of the *awtād*, who is in turn replaced by one of the *abdāl*, and so forth. Many of our rightly guided predecessors (*salaf*) acknowledged their existence, as Imam al-Suyūṭī proves in his work. I personally asked my own teacher, Murabit al-Hajj, about them, and he said, "While some of these terms are mentioned in Qur'an and hadith, others are not; but their existence has been confirmed by too many of the scholars and saints to deny them."

Transliteration Key

THE TRANSLITERATION CONVENTION used throughout this book represents the Arabic script as follows:

Consonants:

ء	’	د	d	ض	ḍ	ك	k
ب	b	ذ	dh	ط	ṭ	ل	l
ت	t	ر	r	ظ	ẓ	م	m
ث	th	ز	z	ع	ʿ	ن	n
ج	j	س	s	غ	gh	ه	h
ح	ḥ	ش	sh	ف	f	و	w
خ	kh	ص	ṣ	ق	q	ي	y

Short vowels:	ـَ	a	ـُ	u	ـِ	i
Long vowels:	ـَا	ā	ـُو	ū	ـِي	ī
Dipthongs:	ـَو	aw	ـَي	ay		

The definite article is rendered *al-* to preserve the representation of the Arabic script as written, not as pronounced, except where fully inflected expressions are quoted as such. Therefore, *ash-shams* is rendered *al-shams*, unless it appears in a fully inflected verbal expression, such as *wa sh-shamsi wa ḍuḥāhā*. Without inflection, this written expression is rendered *wa al-shams wa ḍuḥāhā*.

The *tā’ marbūṭah* is represented by a final *h*, unless it ends the first term of an *iḍāfah* construction, as in *laylat al-qadr*. Note that the *tā’ marbūṭah* in *ahl al-sunnah wa al-jamāʿah*, for instance, is represented as an *h* because it is not the first term of an *iḍāfah* construction.

Hamzat al-waṣl will only be accounted for whenever preceded by a preposition, never for the definite article *alif-lām*, and will in such cases be indicated by a hyphen. Hence, the phrase *wa-mnun ʿalaynā minnata l-karīmi* indicates *hamzat al-waṣl* with a hyphen in *wa-mnun*, but not in *minnata l-karīmi*.

Words that have entered the English language, such as "hadith," "fatwa," and "imam," are not transliterated or italicized unless rendered in formulaic Arabic expressions or idiomatic phrases.

ﷺ An invocation of God's blessings and peace upon the Prophet Muḥammad: "May God's blessings and peace be upon him."
عليه السلام An invocation of God's peace upon a prophet or angel: "May peace be upon him."
عليهما السلام An invocation of God's peace upon two prophets: "May peace be upon them."
عليهم السلام An invocation of God's peace upon three or more prophets: "May peace be upon them."
رضي الله عنه An invocation of God's contentment with a male companion of the Prophet: "May God be pleased with him."
رضي الله عنها An invocation of God's contentment with a female companion of the Prophet: "May God be pleased with her."
رضي الله عنهما An invocation of God's contentment with two companions of the Prophet: "May God be pleased with them."
رضي الله عنهم An invocation of God's contentment with three or more companions of the Prophet: "May God be pleased with them."

Acknowledgments

I WOULD LIKE to especially thank my indefatigable sister and blessed support, Dr. Aisha Subhani, and her husband Dr. Rehan Ahmed Naqui, for their selfless assistance with this work. Dr. Aisha spent a good deal of time with the original lengthy Introduction, narrowing it down ruthlessly with the help of Syeda Feiza Naqvi. Without that effort, this book would not have come to fruition. May God also reward Safir Ahmed, who has improved so much of my humble efforts to present this tradition in the best light, for his editing, advice, and management of the project. Immense gratitude to the American poet and my friend of thirty years, Muqaddim Daniel Abdal-Hayy Moore. I am, as always, indebted to Abdallateef Whiteman for his artwork and graphic design. A special thanks to Nazim Baksh, who tracked down the photograph for the cover of this book and to the photographer, Mikhail Evstafiev, who kindly gave us permission to use it. I am grateful to Noreen Khan and her family, who have supported this work from afar. Thanks also to Najeeb Hasan and the rest of the staff at Zaytuna College for their support and hard work. Also to Shakir Massoud and Hisham Mahmoud for their diligent work and to Hosai Mojaddidi, the Faruqiyyah, as well as Rusha Abdullateef, Zaynab Salman, and Uzma Fatima Husaini for their efforts.

A special thanks to Imam Zaid Shakir, who is always there to give sound advice, reflection, and comments; and to my teacher and guide, Shaykh Abdallah b. Bayyah, who linked me in the blessed chain of Imam Muḥammad b. Nāṣir on the way to Medina, upon its inhabitants be the best of prayers and peace. To the Fes Singers and Mohammed Bennis for such a powerful rendition of the prayer. To Feraidoon Mojadedi and Fouzan Khan for their continued support and trust. A special thanks also to Dr. Suhail Obaji and his family for their continued support for this work and my efforts. To my sister, Nabila, who started this effort and kept it alive in spite of all the hardships, because she believed in the importance of these messages. To Sīdī Ismail al-Filali, may God reward him for his love, devotion, and true brotherhood, and for bringing this prayer to life for me personally, and for reviving its recitation in Fes. May God bless my teacher, Murabit al-Hajj Ould Fahfu, for his prayer for me, and his blessed wife, Maryam, who passed this last year, for all of her service. To Shaykh Abdal Hayy al-Imrawi, for letting me know how important this prayer is in Moroccan history and tradition. I am grateful to Shaykh Muhammad al-Yaqoubi for his explanation of a few abstruse lines, and to Shaykh Jamal Zahabi for editing the Arabic. Many thanks to sister Aishah Holland for being so patient with the project and for her wonderful calligraphy. And a special note of thanks to her brilliant teacher, Sīdī Mohamed Zakariya, for his beautiful rendition of the sacred hadith that appears at the beginning of this work.

To my mother, Elizabeth, who taught me always to side with the oppressed and to defend them, but never to allow hatred of the oppressors to poison one's heart. I especially want to thank my patient and devoted Liliana, who has never complained in over twenty years of companionship. May God raise her into the highest celestial ranks of those who serve the ones serving the great masters of this way. As Imam al-Buṣayrī said in *al-Hamziyyah*, "If God puts one in the service of a saved one, then that one is saved also." To our Prophet Muḥammad ﷺ, the most felicitous of those who are saved; may we always be in his service and the service of those who serve him. May his way be restored to its original glory.